St. Peter's
Church
School.

Editor
 Tom Finley

Assistant Editor
 Lauren Ajer

Consulting Editors
 Rick Bundschuh
 Marian Wiggins
 Annette Parrish

Contributing Writers
 Carol Bostrom
 Ed Reed

Designed and Illustrated by Tom Finley

All Scripture quotations, unless otherwise indicated, are taken from the *Holy Bible, New International Version*®. *NIV*®. Copyright © 1973, 1978, 1984 by International Bible Society. Used by permission of Zondervan Publishing House. All rights reserved.

NASB—Scripture taken from the *New American Standard Bible,* © 1960, 1962, 1963, 1968, 1971, 1972, 1973, 1975, 1977 by The Lockman Foundation. Used by permission.

Jr. High
BUILDERS

**GROUP BIBLE STUDIES
FOR GRADES 6 TO 9**

THE LIFE AND TIMES
OF JESUS CHRIST

NUMBER 2 IN A SERIES OF 12

Gospel Light

INTRODUCTION: OVERVIEW OF THE PARTS AND PIECES

This book contains everything you need to teach any size group of junior high students about Jesus Christ in Mark's Gospel. Thirteen sessions, with complete session plans for the leader, reproducible classroom worksheets and reproducible take-home papers. Also, thirteen lecture-oriented Bible study outlines based on the same themes, to provide your students with needed reinforcement from a fresh perspective. And—dozens of action games and a section of clip art featuring illustrations to promote your Bible studies and dress up your announcement handbills.

#1-9 Jan-Nov/98 (Jueh Williams) Grades 4-10

Contents

The Parts and Pieces

● The **SESSION PLAN** contains two essential ingredients for a meaningful Bible study all students will enjoy: a commentary section to provide the leader with important biblical information and to set the stage for the lesson; and a lesson plan filled with Bible learning activities to help students retain spiritual truths. **FOR A DETAILED DESCRIPTION, TURN TO PAGE 4.**

FOR A DETAILED DESCRIPTION, TURN TO PAGE 4.

Christ Our Hope

SESSION 8

WHAT THE SESSION IS ABOUT
Christ's predictions of our future

SCRIPTURE STUDIED
Mark 13; John 14:16,17; Romans 8:34; 1 Corinthians 10:13; 2 Timothy 3:16; 1 Peter 3:12; 5:7.

KEY PASSAGE
"At that time men will see the Son of Man coming in clouds with great power and glory." Mark 13:26

AIMS OF THE SESSION
During this session your learners will:
1. Study Christ's ___
2. E ___ ___ ions.

INSIGHTS FOR THE LEADER

Mark 13 is the biblical basis for this session. This chapter records an occasion when Jesus warned His followers about a number of upcoming difficulties, and gave them directions for responding to these events. He also spoke of his own return and urged His disciples to watch and be ready for His coming.

This session will not attempt to draw a hard, fast time line of events or reveal all hidden mysteries of the end times. Rather, it will focus primarily on one fact: Jesus is coming. Knowledge of the promised return of Christ is to be an encouragement to His followers who may be immersed in problems and difficulties in their life on earth. We know that some day we will be released from our daily struggle with our own sinful natures, with Satan's efforts to destroy us, and with the influences of the world. We look forward to enjoying fellowship with our Lord ___

Knowing how a crisis will end takes the threat away; and we know that God has already determined how He will end the struggles of human history.

The Bible
Jesus provides hope and encouragement for today through a wide variety of means available until His return. Students will look at just a few of the many ways in which He helps His people. One way is through the provision of the Word. "All Scripture is God-breathed and is useful for teaching, rebuking, correcting and training in righteousness, so that the man of God may be thoroughly equipped for every good work" (2 Tim. 3:16). The Word ___ what we need in order ___. The ___ teaches ___

The **STUDENT WORKSHEET,** called the **Compass,** allows the student to learn by doing rather than just sitting and listening. Photocopy as many sheets as you need. **SEE PAGE 6 FOR COMPLETE DETAILS.**

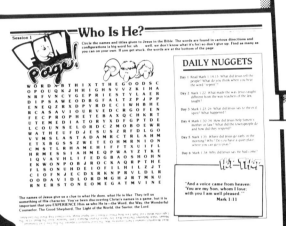

SESSION 2
COMPASS

PART 1: JESUS' TEMPTATIONS

Satan tempted Jesus to do what?	What would Jesus gain (what did Satan promise)?	Why would it be wrong?	How did Jesus respond?

•Group A Read Matthew 4:1-4

•Group B Read Matthew 4:5-7

•Group C Read Matthew 4:8-11

PART 2: PEOPLE TODAY

	What would be a good response?

Using the graffiti you have been given, fill in the columns as they relate to a person your age.

The **TEACHING RESOURCE PAGE** provides necessary items such as short stories or case studies when required by the **Session Plan.** Most **Session Plans** have no **Teaching Resource Page.** **FOR DETAILS, SEE PAGE 7.**

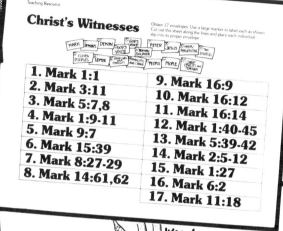

Teaching Resource

Christ's Witnesses

Obtain 17 envelopes. Use a large marker to label each as shown. Cut out this sheet along the lines and place each individual slip into its proper envelope.

1. Mark 1:1	9. Mark 16:9
2. Mark 3:11	10. Mark 16:12
3. Mark 5:7,8	11. Mark 16:14
4. Mark 1:9-11	12. Mark 1:40-45
5. Mark 9:7	13. Mark 5:39-42
6. Mark 15:39	14. Mark 2:5-12
7. Mark 8:27-29	15. Mark 1:27
8. Mark 14:61,62	16. Mark 6:2
	17. Mark 11:18

Session 1
Who Is He?

Circle the names and titles given to Jesus in the Bible. The words are found in various directions and configurations (a big word for, uh well, we don't know what it's for) so don't give up. Find as many as you can on your own. If you get stuck, the words are at the bottom of the page.

DAILY NUGGETS

Day 1: Read Mark 1:14,15. What did Jesus tell the people? What do you think when you hear the word "repent"?

Day 2: Mark 1:22. What made the way Jesus taught different from the way teachers of the law taught?

Day 3: Mark 1:23-28. What did Jesus say to the evil spirit? What happened?

Day 4: Mark 1:30-34. How did Jesus help Simon's mother-in-law? What did the townspeople do and how did they respond?

Day 5: Mark 1:35. Where did Jesus go early in the morning? Why? Do you have a quiet place where you can go to pray?

Day 6: Mark 1:38. Who did Jesus say He had come?

"And a voice came from heaven: 'You are my Son, whom I love; with you I am well pleased.'"
Mark 1:11

The names of Jesus give us a clue to what He does, what He is like. They tell us something of His character. You've been discovering Christ's names in a game, but it is important that you EXPERIENCE Him as who He is—the Word, the Way, the Wonderful Counselor, the Good Shepherd, the Light of the World, the Savior, the Lord.

The **TAKE-HOME PAPER,** called the **Fun Page,** features a Bible game (such as a maze or crossword), and daily devotional questions and a memory verse for motivated students. **FOR MORE ABOUT THE FUN PAGE, TURN TO PAGE 8.**

POPSHEET

THE COMPLETE JUNIOR HIGH BIBLE STUDY RESOURCE BOOK #2
© 1987 GL LIGHT FORCE, VENTURA CA 93006

THEME: One of the characteristics of Christ: His authority.

Session 1

BIBLE STUDY OUTLINE

Read Mark 6:1-7 to your listeners. As time allows, make these points:

• Jesus was teaching in His hometown, Nazareth, at the synagogue. The synagogue was the center of religious education, and Jesus would often teach there. The people were amazed because He taught with authority, not like the usual teachers (refer to Mark 1:21,22).

• The word "authority," in this case, means that Jesus' words had the ring of truth, wisdom, and the ability to motivate and change the lives of the hearers. That is still true today, and why we make no apology for teaching the Bible to you—it is Christ's word, and it can radically change your life by changing your attitudes and point of view. As Paul said: "I am not ashamed of the gospel, because it is the power of God for the salvation of everyone who believes" (Rom. 1:16).

• But the people were offended (Mark 6:2,3) because they thought He was just another laborer from their neighborhood—what gave Him the right to perform miracles and change lives? Of course we know His right came from God. That's another reason we teach the Bible. It's not just sound teaching, it's God's teaching. There are other books of wisdom, I suppose, but only this one comes from God.

• Because few people in His hometown accepted Him, Jesus could only do a few miracles there. In verse 6, it says that Jesus was amazed at their lack of faith. The Bible records only two times when Jesus was amazed—once here for unbelief and once in Luke 7:9 when He was amazed at a Roman centurion's faith. Obviously, Jesus is very concerned about faith or lack of faith. We should be too, still another reason we teach the Bible is stated in Romans 10:17: "Faith comes from hearing the message, and the message is heard through the word of Christ."

• Happily, many people did accept Jesus' teaching. In verse 6 we see that Jesus decided to take His message elsewhere. That message continued to grow and spread, still changing lives today.

TRUE STORY: CHRIST CHANGES A LIFE

We recommend that you relate your own personal testimony of how Christ's powerful teaching has changed your life. If you have recently done that, tell the story of someone you know. If the story you tell is extraordinary (e.g., from face down in the gutter to born again), be sure your students understand that Christ works in every Christian's life, that not always in "hair raising" ways.

Stress the fact that reading the Bible is the key to a changed life because the Bible is God's authoritative Word.

DISCUSSION QUESTIONS

1. Why didn't the other teachers of Jesus' day teach with authority?
2. What sets the Bible apart from other books of good teaching? How often should we read the Bible? What do you do if your Bible is hard to read or a bit dull?
3. Why do you suppose the people in Jesus' hometown didn't have much faith in Him? Do you think it's because they didn't know the real Jesus? Why do people today lack faith?
4. If you think your faith is a bit lacking, what can you do about it?

THE COMPLETE JUNIOR HIGH BIBLE STUDY RESOURCE BOOK #2

Some fun relay races.

GAMES & THINGS

SOCK IT TO ME

...use his or her sock hand to touch the sock. No player can use his hand or any other part. It is not difficult to pass the sock in this manner... battle it can be a lot of fun. (For more difficulty, try passing the sock to hand.)

...ams up single file as a race, or have teams seated at tables.

THAT'S USING YOUR HEAD

...of masking tape for two strips of double sided tape on an 8½ x 11 inch sheet of paper. ...ration. Do this for several sheets of paper, at least one for each player (or more than one if you have more than one turn).

Put the sheets on the floor in front of the teams. At the signal to start, the first player on each team is to stick the paper to the top of his or her head by bending over (no hands on the paper), run to the far wall and stick the paper to the wall. The tape will stick to most wall surfaces better than it sticks to hair. Then the players run back to their teams and tag the next players who repeat the sequence. Caution players not to hit the wall at too high a speed!

WAH!

ICE CREAM SOCIAL

LOOK OUT MOMS!

VALENTINES DAY

The **POPSHEET** is a lecture-oriented version of the **Session Plan,** based on a different portion of the Scriptures. Use it as an alternative to the **Session Plan,** at another meeting later in the week, or combine it with the **Session Plan** as you see fit.

The **Popsheet** features **GAMES AND THINGS,** dozens of action games for your students to enjoy. **PAGE 10 CONTAINS DETAILS.**

The **CLIP ART AND OTHER GOODIES** section at the back of the book contains art and special charts you can use to promote your studies. **SEE PAGE 12 FOR COMPLETE INFORMATION.**

THE SESSION PLANS

How to squeeze the most out of each Bible study.

● **Every Session Plan contains the following features:**

1. INTRODUCTORY INFORMATION

WHAT THE SESSION IS ABOUT states the main thrust of the lesson.

Your students will examine all verses listed in **SCRIPTURE STUDIED.**

The **KEY PASSAGE** is also the memory verse given on the **Fun Page** take-home paper.

AIMS OF THE SESSION is what you hope to achieve during class time. You may wish to privately review these after class as a measure of your success.

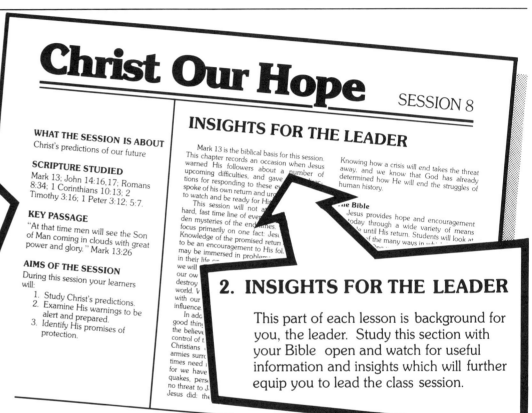

Christ Our Hope
SESSION 8

WHAT THE SESSION IS ABOUT
Christ's predictions of our future

SCRIPTURE STUDIED
Mark 13; John 14:16,17; Romans 8:34; 1 Corinthians 10:13; 2 Timothy 3:16; 1 Peter 3:12; 5:7.

KEY PASSAGE
"At that time men will see the Son of Man coming in clouds with great power and glory." Mark 13:26

AIMS OF THE SESSION
During this session your learners will:
1. Study Christ's predictions.
2. Examine His warnings to be alert and prepared.
3. Identify His promises of protection.

INSIGHTS FOR THE LEADER

Mark 13 is the biblical basis for this session. This chapter records an occasion when Jesus warned His followers about a number of upcoming difficulties, and gave [...] tions for responding to these ev[...] spoke of his own return and ur[...] to watch and be ready for His [...]

This session will not a[...] hard, fast time line of ev[...] den mysteries of the end [...] focus primarily on one fact: Jesu[...] Knowledge of the promised return [...] to be an encouragement to His fol[...] may be immersed in problem[...] in their life or [...] we will [...] our ow[...] destroy [...] world. V[...] with our [...] influence. [...] In add[...] good thing[...] the believe[...] control of t[...] Christians [...] armies surr[...] times need [...] for we have [...] quakes, pers[...] no threat to J[...] Jesus did: the[...]

Knowing how a crisis will end takes the threat away, and we know that God has already determined how He will end the struggles of human history.

[Th]e Bible
Jesus provides hope and encouragement [...] today through a wide variety of means [...] until His return. Students will look at [...] the many ways in [...]

2. INSIGHTS FOR THE LEADER

This part of each lesson is background for you, the leader. Study this section with your Bible open and watch for useful information and insights which will further equip you to lead the class session.

—105—

●══**Three things to note about the Session Plan:**══════════════════

One, the **Session Pan** makes heavy use of **Bible learning activities** (BLA's). A Bible learning activity is precisely what it sounds like—an activity students perform to learn about the Bible. Because *action* is employed, the student has a much greater chance of **COMPREHENDING** and **RETAINING** spiritual insights. And because you the leader can see what the student is doing you can readily **MEASURE** the student's comprehension. The BLA allows you to **WALK AROUND THE CLASSROOM** as students work, answering questions or dealing with problem students. Furthermore, it's **EASIER TO TEACH WELL** using BLA's. If you've never used BLA's before, you will quickly find them much simpler to prepare and deliver than a whole session of lecture.

Two, the **Session Plan** provides guided conversation—suggestions on what to say throughout the class time. Notice that the guided conversation is always printed in **BOLD TYPE** in the **Session Plan.** LIGHT TYPE indicates instructions to you, the teacher.

Three, if special or unusual preparation is required before class begins, it will be listed immediately below the title **SESSION PLAN,** under the heading *BEFORE CLASS BEGINS.*

4

3. SESSION PLAN

This heading introduces the step-by-step lesson plan. With careful planning, you can easily tailor each session to the amount of class time you have.

4. ATTENTION GRABBER

Who knows what lurks in the minds of your students as they file into your room? The **Attention Grabber** will stimulate their interest and focus their thinking on the theme of the lesson.

The **Attention Grabber,** as well as other parts of the **Session Plan,** often—but not always—contain an additional alternate activity. These alternates are identified by the titles **"CREATIVE OPTION," "OPTIONAL"** or similar designations. Choose the activity that best suits the needs of your class and fits your time schedule.

5. BIBLE EXPLORATION

The **Bible Exploration** is the heart of your class session because it involves each learner directly in the study of God's Word. It is during this period that you will invite the students to explore and discover **WHAT THE BIBLE SAYS AND MEANS** and to discuss **HOW IT APPLIES TO EACH STUDENT.**

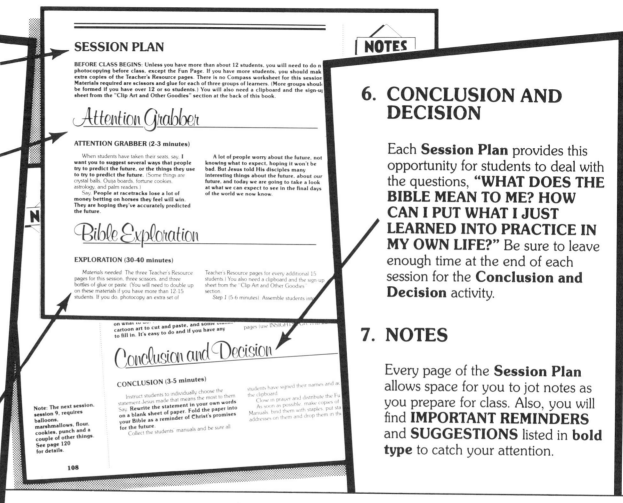

6. CONCLUSION AND DECISION

Each **Session Plan** provides this opportunity for students to deal with the questions, **"WHAT DOES THE BIBLE MEAN TO ME? HOW CAN I PUT WHAT I JUST LEARNED INTO PRACTICE IN MY OWN LIFE?"** Be sure to leave enough time at the end of each session for the **Conclusion and Decision** activity.

7. NOTES

Every page of the **Session Plan** allows space for you to jot notes as you prepare for class. Also, you will find **IMPORTANT REMINDERS** and **SUGGESTIONS** listed in **bold type** to catch your attention.

● Necessary Classroom Supplies

The Session Plan Bible study activities require that you make the following items readily available to students:

- A Bible for each student (Essential!) • Paper and pencils or pens • Scissors
- • Felt markers • Butcher paper for posters • Transparent tape

You, the teacher, will need a chalkboard or overhead projector.

Special requirements will be listed in the NOTES section of the proper Session Plans.

THE COMPASS STUDENT WORKSHEETS

The Compass helps students discover God's Word for themselves.

The page immediately following each **Session Plan** is the **Compass** worksheet for your students. Here's how to use them, in 5 easy steps:

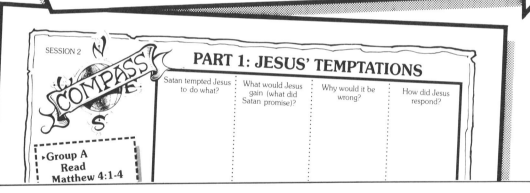

SESSION 2

PART 1: JESUS' TEMPTATIONS

Satan tempted Jesus to do what?	What would Jesus gain (what did Satan promise)?	Why would it be wrong?	How did Jesus respond?

▶Group A
Read
Matthew 4:1-4

● TRY THESE SPECIAL TIPS:

Photocopy all youth group announcements on the reverse side of the **Compass** The **Clip Art and Other Goodies** section at the back of this book will be a big help here.

Use different colored paper from week to week in your copier. If your machine can enlarge, print the worksheets "giant size" once in awhile.

Too much of even a good thing is too much. We suggest that every now and then you hand out blank paper and simply *read* the **Compass** instructions to your students.
Or write the instructions on the chalkboard. Or hand write and copy your own worksheets. Variety is the key.

1. Before class, use your church photocopier to reproduce enough student worksheets for your learners and a few extra for visitors. With rare exception, there is only one **Compass** sheet per session. (You may wish to photocopy all 13 sessions at one time to save trips.)

2. The **Compasses** are generally used throughout each **Session Plan**. The best time to distribute them to students is when the **Session Plan** first calls for their use. Always keep a copy for yourself.

3. Be sure to have **plenty of blank paper** for students' written assignments—the **Compasses** don't have much extra space.

4. It may help to have your students fold their **Compasses** into their Bibles if there is a gap between uses of the worksheet. This will aid you in avoiding the Paper Airplane Syndrome.

5. Collect and save the worksheets at the end of each class. (Do not collect worksheets that contain private confessions to God or the like.) You can follow the progress of your students by examining their work. Parents, too, will want to see what their children are learning.

THE TEACHING RESOURCE PAGES

Special "goodies" to help you teach.

A few sessions require extra "goodies" such as board games or short stories. These are provided by the **Teaching Resource Pages** which follow the **Compass** in the appropriate sessions.

The **Session Plans** and the **Resource Pages** contain complete instructions.

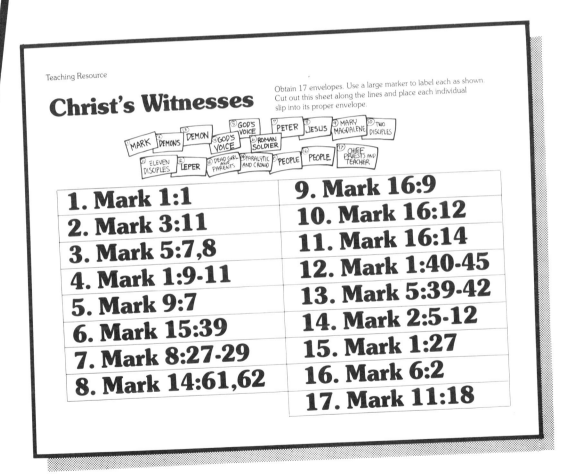

Teaching Resource

Christ's Witnesses

Obtain 17 envelopes. Use a large marker to label each as shown. Cut out this sheet along the lines and place each individual slip into its proper envelope.

1. Mark 1:1	9. Mark 16:9
2. Mark 3:11	10. Mark 16:12
3. Mark 5:7,8	11. Mark 16:14
4. Mark 1:9-11	12. Mark 1:40-45
5. Mark 9:7	13. Mark 5:39-42
6. Mark 15:39	14. Mark 2:5-12
7. Mark 8:27-29	15. Mark 1:27
8. Mark 14:61,62	16. Mark 6:2
	17. Mark 11:18

THE FUN PAGE TAKE-HOME PAPERS

Give your students a treat! The **Fun Page** combines games, memory verses and daily devotional studies into an enjoyable, fun-filled take-home paper.

Features:

Each **Fun Page** contains a Bible game designed to amplify the insights gained in the classroom. Mazes, crosswords, word searches—games ranging from the simple to the extremely challenging.

There's cartoon artwork, informal readability, and humor that your students will welcome.

The **Daily Nuggets** section is a simple six-day devotional based on passages related to the Scriptures studied in class. See "TIPS" for important advice.

The **Hot Thot** memory verse helps students lock the wisdom of God's Word into their minds and hearts.

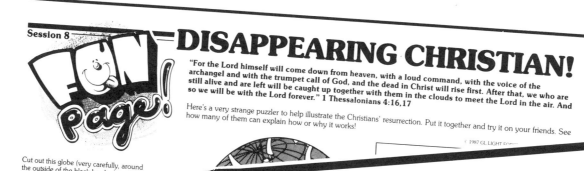

Session 8

DISAPPEARING CHRISTIAN!

"For the Lord himself will come down from heaven, with a loud command, with the voice of the archangel and with the trumpet call of God, and the dead in Christ will rise first. After that, we who are still alive and are left will be caught up together with them in the clouds to meet the Lord in the air. And so we will be with the Lord forever." 1 Thessalonians 4:16,17

Here's a very strange puzzler to help illustrate the Christians' resurrection. Put it together and try it on your friends. See how many of them can explain how or why it works!

© 1987 GL LIGHT FORCE

Cut out this globe (very carefully, around the outside of the black border line) push a tack thro...

TIPS:

You can use the **Fun Page** several ways:

- As a **take-home paper** to extend the classroom into the week. Hand out copies as students leave class.
- As a special **Bible learning activity** during class. (Some of the games would make interesting **Attention Grabbers,** for example.)
- Make it the **focal point of another Bible study.** For instance, if you used the **Session Plan** Sunday morning, you could reinforce the lesson during an informal midweek meeting by involving students in answering the questions in the **Daily Nuggets** section.
- Even absentees can be involved. Put the **Fun Page** into an envelope along with a personal note to that learner who needs a little encouragement.

A word about MOTIVATION:

You won't have any trouble getting your students to play the games on the **Fun Page.** (Just see how many of them are playing the games during church service!) But the **Daily Nuggets** and the **Hot Thot** memory verse can be problems. Here are two ways to motivate students to answer the daily devotional questions and memorize the verse:

1. Start a contest. Award points to those students who complete the assignments, bring friends, and memorize passages. Pick a nice prize such as a free trip to camp and run the contest for about five weeks. (Longer makes for lack of interest.)

2. Combine the assignments with a discipleship class. If you are not personally involved in the discipleship program, give a copy of the **Fun Page** to the leader.

THE POPSHEET LECTURE BIBLE STUDIES

"Pop" these **Popsheets** out of this book and give them to the leader of your youth group's other meetings. Great for an at-home Bible study, a camp retreat, games night or special event.

Youth groups come in all sizes and shapes. So do youth programs. Meetings vary widely in style—ranging from Sunday morning Bible studies with singing and announcements, to deeper discipleship programs for motivated students, to the fun and action of "game nights" with very short Bible messages.

The **Popsheets** offer a good source of creative thinking for whatever type of program you have. **Popsheets** are packed with Bible stories, object lessons, case studies, discussion questions, and fast-paced games aimed at the junior high "squirrel" mentality! Each **Popsheet** covers the same theme as the accompanying **Session Plan,** but the stories, verses, object lessons and case studies are all new and fresh. The advantages?

- For students who attended the **Session Plan** class, a fresh new perspective on the topic. A great way to insure retention.

- For learners who missed the **Session Plan** class, a good way to keep current with the other students. This is a sound method to guarantee that all your youth group members explore every topic in a Bible study series.

- Or use your creativity to replace some of the Bible learning activities in the **Session Plan** with the **Popsheets'** object lessons and short stories.

THEME

The same theme as the accompanying **Session Plan**

BIBLE STUDY OUTLINE

A suggested Bible passage with a list of important points to make during your lecture. The **Bible Study Outline** offers a **basic** lesson plan to stimulate your thinking as you prayerfully prepare your message. **Use your own creativity and ability to "flesh it out."** There is plenty here for outstanding Bible messages your students will enjoy and remember.

Notice that the **Bible Study Outline** contains no **Bible learning activities.** The **Popsheet** is designed to be a short Bible message that you can give at an informal "games night," camp cabin devotional, or what have you.

OBJECT LESSON

Each **Popsheet** has an object lesson, short story, or case study. (A case study is a description of an event or situation a junior high student is likely to face in life.) These add spice to your messages. A good object lesson, for instance, and the spiritual truth it conveys, can be remembered for a lifetime.

DISCUSSION QUESTIONS

You may wish to involve your students in your lectures by asking them about the issues and implications of the Bible study. Feel free to modify or add to the questions to more nearly suit your students' needs.

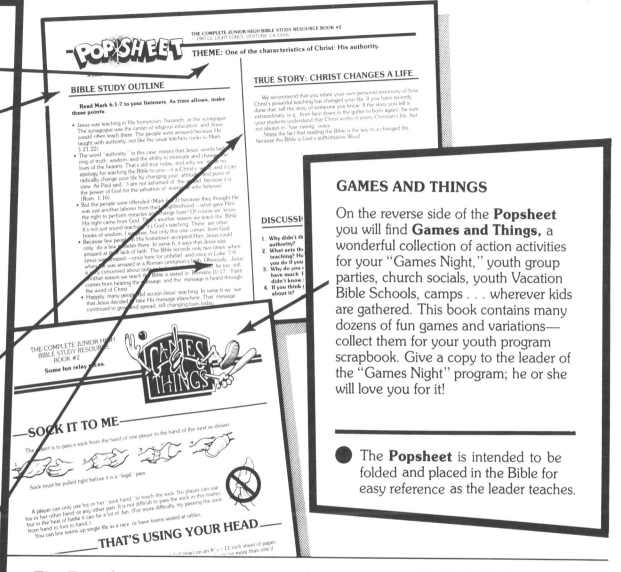

GAMES AND THINGS

On the reverse side of the **Popsheet** you will find **Games and Things,** a wonderful collection of action activities for your "Games Night," youth group parties, church socials, youth Vacation Bible Schools, camps . . . wherever kids are gathered. This book contains many dozens of fun games and variations—collect them for your youth program scrapbook. Give a copy to the leader of the "Games Night" program; he or she will love you for it!

● The **Popsheet** is intended to be folded and placed in the Bible for easy reference as the leader teaches.

The **Popsheet** is an exciting new edition to the **LIGHT FORCE** line of junior high Bible study materials. It contains truly useful features that will help make your informal Bible study meetings of keen interest to your learners.

The **Popsheet** is for you to use. Take advantage of it. Use it as an aid to your Bible study preparation and game plans. You'll be glad you did.

INTRODUCTION TO CLIP ART

Good news for those who can't draw.

If you want your class or youth group to increase in size—and who doesn't—you'll welcome the **Clip Art and Other Goodies** section found at the rear of this book. Create your own terrific monthly youth group activity calendars, announcement sheets and posters. It's fun and easy! Simply follow the tips and techniques in the Clip Art and Other Goodies section; you'll produce great "promo pieces" that will attract kids to your Bible studies and other events.

Remember: Even if you can't draw cartoons, with the right promotional clip art you can draw kids.

CLIP ART AND OTHER GOODIES

The following pages contain all sorts of fun, high quality clip art. Put it to good use: brighten up your youth group's mail outs, bulletins, posters, and overhead transparencies. Cut 'em out, paste 'em up, run 'em off, and there you have it!

WAH!

ICE CREAM SOCIAL

VALENTINES DAY

BIBLE

BIBLE

POOL PARTY

POOL PARTY

You'll be happy to know that the LIGHT FORCE publishes two great clip art books: the original YOUTH WORKER'S CLIP ART BOOK and the famous SON OF CLIP ART! Both books are available at your local Christian supply store, or write   THE LIGHT FORCE
P.O. BOX 6309
OXNARD, CA 93031

WANT TO PRODUCE GREAT PROMOTIONAL MATERIAL? TURN THE PAGE FOR EASY INSTRUCTIONS.

181

Who Is He?

WHAT THE SESSION IS ABOUT

Mark reveals that Jesus is the Son of God, the Messiah, a miracle worker, able to forgive sin, and an authoritative teacher.

SCRIPTURE STUDIED

Mark 1:1,9-11,27,40-45; 2:5-12; 3:11,12; 5:7,8,39-42; 6:2; 8:27-30; 9:7; 11:18; 14:61,62; 15:39; 16:9,12,14.

KEY PASSAGE

"And a voice came from heaven: 'You are my Son, whom I love; with you I am well pleased.'" Mark 1:11

AIMS OF THE SESSION

During this session your learners will:

1. Study many of the characteristics of Christ from the book of Mark.
2. Discuss the importance of Christ's characteristics for people today.
3. Choose one characteristic and determine a personal response to it.

INSIGHTS FOR THE LEADER

When Jesus walked the earth, He touched the lives of thousands of people. The book of Mark records the reactions of many of these people, including Christ's disciples, sick people, high priests, teachers of the rabbinical law, and even evil spirits. By examining these responses, your students can build an interesting composite picture of who Jesus is and what He came to do. An accurate understanding of Jesus' identity and purpose is essential to your students' spiritual development.

God's Son

The very first verse in Mark's gospel tells us the view that Mark held: "The beginning of the gospel about Jesus Christ, the Son of God." Not only does Mark claim that Jesus is the promised Christ—the Messiah, the One sent from God to act as bridge between God and humanity—but also that He is God's very Son.

Even the enemies of Christ recognized His intimate relation to the Father: "Whenever the evil spirits saw him, they fell down before him and cried out, 'You are the Son of God'" (Mark 3:11). A specific example of this is given in Mark 5:7,8.

And Mark 15:39 tells us about a Roman soldier who, amazed at the way Jesus behaved as He died, proclaimed, "Surely this man was the Son of God!" (Mark 15:39).

But the most unimpeachable testimony of all comes from God Himself. Twice in Mark God's voice rang out from heaven, saying, "You are my Son" (see Mark 1:9-11 and 9:7).

The significance of Christ's relation to God is that He is actually God. He has all the power and authority of that position. Your students can tap into that amazing power by drawing close to the Son of God.

The Christ

In addition to Mark's statement that Jesus is the Christ (1:1), we find recorded Peter's famous confession: "You are the Christ" (Mark 8:29). This is no small insight on Peter's part. All of Israel was either waiting expectantly for the Messiah to come, or despairing at His perceived lateness. But the Messiah they expected was to be a triumphant King, not the son of a lowly carpenter.

We now know that Jesus will someday visibly conquer and rule the world. But at the time Peter spoke, he had to go on faith. What were Peter's feelings as he spoke these words? Perhaps he felt hope and desire as much as conviction.

But Peter and Mark are not the only ones who made the claim. When asked by the high priest, "Are you the Christ, the Son of the Blessed One?" Jesus said, "I am . . . . And you will see the Son of Man sitting at the right hand of the Mighty One and coming on the clouds of heaven" (Mark 14:61,62). All of these things Jesus said, including the peculiar gram-

mar He used for "I am," were reserved only for the Messiah. To say them, Jesus was either the Messiah or a terrible blasphemer. It was this statement that caused the high priest and the others to condemn Jesus to death.

Why was a Messiah needed so badly in those days—and still today? Because the Messiah was the One sent from God to reconcile people to God. He was to make the two one. Your students must be made aware that no mere human is good enough or strong enough to work his or her way to God. Only Jesus the Christ can draw us to Him.

The Risen Christ

A dead Messiah is useless. That is why it is important to review the testimonies of Mary Magdalene and several disciples who saw, in separate incidents, the risen Lord Jesus. You and your learners will examine these incidents during class time as you study Mark 16:9,12,14. You will want to stress the fact that Jesus is perfectly alive and well today. Christianity is not a dead religion, but a living faith based on a living God—a faith which can meet the needs of and forever change even the most hardhearted junior high student.

The Miracle Worker

Christ demonstrated the reality of His claims by performing miraculous signs, observed by many. In Mark 1:40-45, Jesus healed a leper who then went out to spread the good news (against Christ's instructions!) of his cure. Mark 5:39-42 records the astonishment of those who witnessed Jesus raising a dead girl to life. And Mark 2:5-12 tells us about the crowd's reaction to the healing of a paralyzed man.

Again, our Lord is not dead nor weak. He worked miracles then and He works them now. If you have had a personal experience with the miraculous, you may wish to make a note to yourself to tell your story to your learners when you begin to discuss this part of the lesson. Young ears love to hear and young minds long remember true stories of Christ's miraculous power.

The Forgiver of Sin

This same passage recording the healing of the paralyzed man makes it clear that modern Christians have too long ignored the horrible spiritual costs of sin. Sin destroys. It destroys our effectiveness on this planet by cutting our direct line to God.

But Jesus is far stronger than sin. He abolishes it by forgiving us. Point out to your students that a few minutes spent in prayerful confession each day can radically transform their usefulness to God and to this world.

The Authoritative Teacher

The best teacher is the one who teaches with authority. Authority comes from personal involvement, not repetition of someone else's stories or experiences. Jesus could teach the truth with authority because He is truth (see John 14:6).

His authoritative words shocked and excited His listeners. Read the words of one crowd of witnesses: "The people were all so amazed that they asked each other, 'What is this? A new teaching—and with authority!' " These words of astonishment are found in Mark 1:27. Again in Mark 6:2 we see a bewildered crowd: "When the Sabbath came, he began to teach in the synagogue, and many who heard him were amazed."

Today, the best Christian teaching comes from those who simply expound the Word of God to those who need to hear. There is no substitute for Bible study. Christ's words changed lives then and His words change lives now.

If it seems to you that your students may be overwhelmed by the sheer number of passages studied in this session, do not fret. Each learner will gain genuine and lasting insight into the character of Jesus, the Son of God, risen Christ, miracle worker, forgiver, and great teacher. Also, many of these same passages will be covered in greater detail in coming class times. Although junior high students can seem frustratingly unmoved by the Word of God, keep your eyes open. As time goes by, lasting decisions will be made.

SESSION PLAN

BEFORE CLASS BEGINS: You will need some envelopes prepared as described on the "Christ's Witnesses" Teaching Resource page, which is after the Compass Student Worksheet following this SESSION PLAN.

Attention Grabber

ATTENTION GRABBER (1-2 minutes)

Choose a student (one who is well liked and not easily embarrassed) to come forward and stand with you at the head of the class.

Say, **Who are you? What is your name?** When the student answers, say something like, **Are you really? I'm not sure I believe you! I want you to prove that you are who you say you are. Show me some ID.** Most students don't carry genuine identification cards; if yours has one, continue with your act of disbelief by demanding still more proof.

Your student will probably tell you that many of the people present can back up his or her claims. (If the student doesn't hit on this idea, suggest it yourself.) Say, **If you can vouch for this person,** **raise your hand.** Graciously accept the testimony of the crowd, apologize to the student and have him or her sit down.

Move on to the EXPLORATION by saying something like this: **Because so many of you are willing to testify that [name of student] is who he says he is, I must accept his word as truth. I'd be a fool if I didn't. The overwhelming majority of you back him up.**

This week we begin a study of Jesus Christ—who He is, what He's like, what He said and did, and so forth. Today we'll explore who Jesus is, based on the testimony of many witnesses as recorded in the book of Mark.

Bible Exploration

EXPLORATION (25-35 minutes)

Materials needed: Seventeen envelopes; the "Christ's Witnesses" Teaching Resource page that you'll find after The Compass student worksheet following this SESSION PLAN. Prepare the envelopes as described on the Teaching Resource.
Step 1 (10-15 minutes): Distribute the

envelopes, one to a student. (If necessary, each student can have more than one.) Say, **I'm handing out "Witness Envelopes." These envelopes are labeled with the name or names of people who saw Jesus, people who witnessed what He did and who can vouch for who He is and what He is like. You'll notice that some of you are demons (how appropriate!), some are disciples, one is a dead girl, some are sick people and so on. We have so many envelopes because there are so many people who saw Jesus and can testify to His reality.**

Have the student with envelope number one identify him or herself (by reading the envelope's label; in this case Mark). Then the student should tear open the envelope and read the slip inside. Have all students turn in their Bibles to that passage and have "Mark" or another volunteer read it aloud as others follow along.

When the reading is completed ask your class what the witness Mark teaches us about Jesus. In this case, Mark tells us that Jesus is the Son of God. As each witness in turn presents his or her

testimony, write the name of the witness and what is taught about Jesus on the chalkboard.

Step 2 (15-20 minutes): Distribute copies of The Compass and draw your learners' attention to "The Importance of Christ's Characteristics."

Tell students to work individually (or in small groups if you prefer) to complete the assignment. Say, **You may look at what I've written on the chalkboard as you work.**

When all have finished, lead a discussion based on the "WHY IT'S IMPORTANT" column of the assignment, using the following situations and questions to stimulate your students' thinking (add your own questions and comments to guide the discussion):

1. **Think of a friend you have who has an unhappy home life. Without mentioning your friend's name, describe what sort of miraculous help Jesus could offer if He showed up at your friend's house today.**
2. **Name a few things that many of your friends in school could learn from Jesus that would make them better people and cause them to enjoy life more.**
3. **When we speak of Jesus as being the "bridge between God and man," we usually think of salvation. Name some other important ways that Jesus brings us close to God each day.**
4. **What must we do to have our sins forgiven? (See 1 John 1:9.)**
5. **Sometimes on the news we hear about ambassadors from other countries visiting our own. What is the purpose of an ambassador and how does this relate to the fact that Jesus is God's Son?**
6. **Have you ever had a pet die? Describe some of the differences between a living animal and a dead one. How valuable do you think Christianity would be if Christ was dead? What are some of the advantages to having a living Lord today?**

Thank the students for their insights.

Conclusion and Decision

CONCLUSION (5-10 minutes):

Direct attention to the "Dork Tracy" section of the worksheet and explain, **You are to work individually to complete the detective's final report on Jesus Christ. You are the detective, you have heard the witnesses. When you get to the last part that says, "BECAUSE OF WHO JESUS IS, I'M GOING TO" write down a specific action you would like to take, such as giving Him control over a particular area of your life, or telling a certain friend about Him, or spending more time with Him. No one will look at what you write.**

If some students finish early, give them copies of the Fun Page take-home paper. Point out the "Who Is He?" word-search puzzle and allow students to work on it quietly while others finish the "detective report."

Close in prayer. Distribute the rest of the Fun Pages and encourage everyone to work the "Daily Nuggets" and "Hot Thot" at home.

SUGGESTION: To help motivate your students to do the "Daily Nuggets" and to memorize the Bible verse, give each student a copy of the "Daily Vitamins" chart. You'll find it in the "Clip Art and Other Goodies" section. Spend a few minutes going over the chart with your students before they leave.

NOTES

You can help your students develop a habit of daily Bible reading and memorization by giving them the "Daily Vitamins" chart. See page 187 for details.

Your students may wish to see this solution to the Fun Page puzzle.

(If you like, write the solution on an extra copy of the Fun Page and pin it to your classroom bulletin board.)

Note: The next session, Session 2, requires preparation as described on page 29. You will need special materials for the EXPLORATION and the CREATIVE OPTION.

17

SESSION 1

The Importance of Christ's Characteristics

Based on what you've learned today, use a pencil to connect the WITNESSES in the left column to WHAT THEY SAID about Jesus in the middle. Then draw lines from WHAT THEY SAID to WHY IT'S IMPORTANT, picking the ones you think match.

WITNESSES	WHAT THEY SAID	WHY IT'S IMPORTANT
Mark	Jesus is the Son of God	He can work miracles in our lives today
Peter	Jesus is the Christ (The bridge between God and man.)	He can teach us to live wisely and well
Disciples		
Demon or demons		
Jesus Himself		
Leper	Jesus is risen and alive	He is the way to God
Chief Priests		
Mary Magdalene	Jesus works miracles	He can set us right with God
God's voice		
Roman soldier	Jesus forgives sins	He has the power of His Father
Paralytic and crowd		
Dead girl and family	Jesus teaches with authority	He is still alive and active
People		

Dork Tracy Detective Agency

Write your personal reaction to who Jesus is and what He can do for you, if you let Him.

■ SUBJECT:

■ WHO JESUS IS (write what the witnesses said):

■ BECAUSE OF WHO JESUS IS, I RECOMMEND THAT PEOPLE MY AGE SHOULD:

■ BECAUSE OF WHO JESUS IS, I'M GOING TO:

SIGNATURE _____ DATE _____

Christ's Witnesses

Obtain 17 envelopes. Use a large marker to label each as shown. Cut out this sheet along the lines and place each individual slip into its proper envelope.

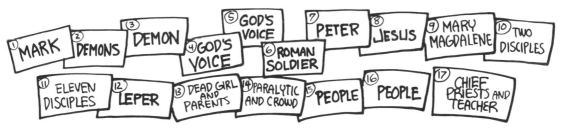

1. Mark 1:1	9. Mark 16:9
2. Mark 3:11	10. Mark 16:12
3. Mark 5:7,8	11. Mark 16:14
4. Mark 1:9-11	12. Mark 1:40-45
5. Mark 9:7	13. Mark 5:39-42
6. Mark 15:39	14. Mark 2:5-12
7. Mark 8:27-29	15. Mark 1:27
8. Mark 14:61,62	16. Mark 6:2
	17. Mark 11:18

Who Is He?

Circle the names and titles given to Jesus in the Bible. The words are found in various directions and configurations (a big word for, uh . . . well, we don't know what it's for) so don't give up. Find as many as you can on your own. If you get stuck, the words are at the bottom of the page.

```
W O R D A B T H I X T T H E G O O D S C
O P O U Q K J H H I G H S V V Z K I H A
N R F V N C Y G E P R I E S T Y L A E R
D I P S A W E O D B G F A L T Z P J P P
E N E Q Z R X D P Y R D E C I W H B H E
R C A S A V I O U R V E D C R G O F E N
F E C P R O P H E T E B A X Q C H K R T
U T E M E D I A T O R Y X D F G P T D E
L C O U N S E L O R D C Z M O B O E W R
W A T H E U F D J E S U S Z R F D L G O
V V M S L A S T A D A M R C T R L A H M
E T X B G S S Z W E T E O H M R N I O N
C M S T L R H A M E H I E F T X U I F L
H R M E S S I A H M E Q P W A Y Z T K E
I Q V A V H L I F E D G B A O S H O H N
E K W O N P O B J R O C K A Q R P T H E
F L S O N U H D E I O F I L H I L Z J T
C I O L N J E C D X R K N P R V L D L R
O O D A V I D L O R D M G H J R T M K U
R N E R S T O N E O M E G A T M V I N E
```

The names of Jesus give us a clue to what He does, what He is like. They tell us something of His character. You've been discovering Christ's names in a game, but it is important that you EXPERIENCE Him as who He is—the Word, the Way, the Wonderful Counselor, The Good Shepherd, The Light of the World, the Savior, the Lord.

Word, Wonderful Counselor, Chief Cornerstone, Way, The Good Shepherd, Carpenter, The True Vine, Lord, Emmanuel, Messiah, Shiloh, Redeemer, The Door, Rock, Life, Savior, Prophet, Mediator, Lamb, Nazarene, Jesus, The Bread of Life, The Light of the World, God, Truth, Lion, King, Prince of Peace, Lord, Alpha Omega, Son of David, High Priest, The Last Adam.

DAILY NUGGETS

Day 1 Read Mark 1:14,15. What did Jesus tell the people? What do you think when you hear the word "repent"?

Day 2 Mark 1:22. What made the way Jesus taught different from the way teachers of the law taught?

Day 3 Mark 1:23-26. What did Jesus say to the evil spirit? What happened?

Day 4 Mark 1:30-34. How did Jesus help Simon's mother-in-law? What did the townspeople do and how did they respond?

Day 5 Mark 1:35. Where did Jesus go early in the morning? Why? Do you have a quiet place where you can go to pray?

Day 6 Mark 1:38. Why did Jesus say He had come?

"And a voice came from heaven: 'You are my Son, whom I love; with you I am well pleased.'"

Mark 1:11

THEME: One of the characteristics of Christ: His authority.

Session 1

BIBLE STUDY OUTLINE

Read Mark 6:1-7 to your listeners. As time allows, make these points:

- Jesus was teaching in His hometown, Nazareth, at the synagogue. The synagogue was the center of religious education, and Jesus would often teach there. The people were amazed because He taught with authority, not like the usual teachers (refer to Mark 1:21,22).
- The word "authority," in this case, means that Jesus' words had the ring of truth, wisdom, and the ability to motivate and change the lives of the hearers. That's still true today, and why we make no apology for teaching the Bible to you—it is Christ's word, and it can radically change your life by changing your attitudes and point of view. As Paul said, "I am not ashamed of the gospel, because it is the power of God for the salvation of everyone who believes" (Rom. 1:16).
- But the people were offended (Mark 6:2,3) because they thought He was just another laborer from their neighborhood—what gave Him the right to perform miracles and change lives? Of course we know His right came from God. That's another reason we teach the Bible: It's not just sound teaching, it's God's teaching. There are other books of wisdom, I suppose, but only this one comes from God.
- Because few people in His hometown accepted Him, Jesus could only do a few miracles there. In verse 6, it says that Jesus was amazed at their lack of faith. The Bible records only two times when Jesus was amazed—once here for unbelief, and once in Luke 7:9, when He was amazed at a Roman centurion's faith. Obviously, Jesus is very concerned about faith or lack of faith. We should be too; still another reason we teach the Bible is stated in Romans 10:17: "Faith comes from hearing the message, and the message is heard through the word of Christ."
- Happily, many people did accept Jesus' teaching. In verse 6 we see that Jesus decided to take His message elsewhere. That message continued to grow and spread, still changing lives today.

TRUE STORY: CHRIST CHANGES A LIFE

We recommend that you relate your own personal testimony of how Christ's powerful teaching has changed your life. If you have recently done that, tell the story of someone you know. If the story you tell is extraordinary (e.g., from face down in the gutter to born again), be sure your students understand that Christ works in every Christian's life, but not always in "hair-raising" ways.

Stress the fact that reading the Bible is the key to a changed life, because the Bible is God's authoritative Word.

DISCUSSION QUESTIONS

1. **Why didn't the other teachers of Jesus' day teach with authority?**
2. **What sets the Bible apart from other books of good teaching? How often should we read the Bible? What do you do if your Bible is hard to read or a bit dull?**
3. **Why do you suppose the people in Jesus' hometown didn't have much faith in Him? Do you think it's because they didn't know the *real* Jesus? Why do people today lack faith?**
4. **If you think your faith is a bit lacking, what can you do about it?**

Some fun relay races.

SOCK IT TO ME

The object is to pass a sock from the hand of one player to the hand of the next as shown:

 1.

 2.

 3.

 4.

Sock must be pulled tight before it is a "legal" pass.

A player can only use his or her "sock hand" to touch the sock. No player can use his or her other hand or any other part. It is not difficult to pass the sock in this matter, but in the heat of battle it can be a lot of fun. (For more difficulty, try passing the sock from hand to hand.)
You can line teams up single file as a race, or have teams seated at tables.

THAT'S USING YOUR HEAD

Place two loops of masking tape (or two strips of double-sided tape) on an 8½ × 11-inch sheet of paper, as shown in the illustration. Do this for several sheets of paper, at least one per player (or more than one if you want players to have more than one turn).

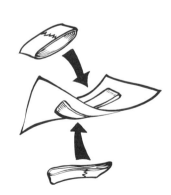

Put the sheets on the floor in front of the teams. At the signal to start, the first player on each team is to stick the paper to the top of his or her head by bending over (no hands on the paper), run to the far wall and stick the paper to the wall. The tape will stick to most wall surfaces better than it sticks to hair. Then the players run back to their teams and tag the next players who repeat the sequence. Caution players not to hit the wall at too high a speed!

Temptation

INSIGHTS FOR THE LEADER

WHAT THE SESSION IS ABOUT
The way Jesus handled temptation is the way we should handle it.

SCRIPTURE STUDIED
Matthew 4:1-11; Mark 1:12,13.

KEY PASSAGE
"For we do not have a high priest who is unable to sympathize with our weaknesses, but we have one who has been tempted in every way, just as we are—yet was without sin." Hebrews 4:15

AIMS OF THE SESSION
During this session your learners will:
1. Discover how Jesus responded to temptation.
2. List some ways young people are tempted.
3. Turn one area of temptation over to the Lord.

This session will enable your students to examine the temptation experience of Christ in the wilderness and compare it to their own struggles with temptation. They will discover a Christ who, though He is God, experienced every aspect of human life including the struggle to overcome evil. He "has been tempted in every way, just as we are—yet was without sin" (Heb. 4:15). And they will discover the common element in His responses to temptations—His use of Scripture.

Before looking more closely at Christ's experience, we should define the word "temptation." The biblical sense of the word was to put someone to the test. This might occur to demonstrate the person's qualities and to strengthen him or her; or it might be for the purpose of showing the person's weaknesses or trapping him or her into doing something wrong. In the last two or three hundred years, however, the meaning of the word has been limited to the negative connotation.

Mark touches the temptation of Christ only briefly (see Mark 1:12,13), but the subject is so important to the Christian life that it justifies a close look at the parallel passage in Matthew 4:1-11. As your learners study the passage, they will discover the nature of temptation, what Christ would have "gained" by yielding, why it was wrong, and how Christ responded. Jesus made three answers to Satan's ploys.

Answer Number One: Listen to God
The first temptation was Satan's taunt, "If you are the Son of God, tell these stones to become bread" (Matt. 4:3). If Jesus had yielded, He would have satisfied a basic physical need—in this case, the need for food. (He had been fasting for forty days.) There is nothing wrong with needing food or eating, since God has made us that way. But under the circumstances, it would have been wrong for Jesus to turn stones into bread in order to meet that need. It would have been a wrong use of His power as God. He came to serve others (us), not to make life easy for Himself. If Jesus had done what Satan demanded, He would have aborted His whole mission to earth, as He would have been meeting His need at our expense. Remind students that if Jesus had turned stones into bread, we would not be able to identify with Him as our "high priest . . . who has been tempted in every way, just as we are—yet . . . without sin" (Heb. 4:15). We do not have the ability to turn stones into bread when we are famished. In addition, the act of turning stones into bread would have been a denial of God's ability to provide for Him.

Instead of yielding, Jesus quoted Scripture. He said, "It is written: 'Man does not live on bread alone, but on every word that comes from the mouth of God' " (Matt. 4:4). He

NOTES

chose a Scripture appropriate to the situation. And He said no to the temptation.

Living on God's Word is the first key to unlocking the chains of temptation. Listening to what God says rather than what Satan says—not just now and then, but habitually—is the logical first step in resisting the Devil. Encourage your students to get to know their Bibles well. The "Daily Nuggets" and "Hot Thot" sections of the Fun Page will help develop good habits.

Answer Number Two: Do What God Says

The next thing Satan did was to take Jesus into the city of Jerusalem and to the highest point of the Temple. Then he said, "If you are the Son of God, . . . throw yourself down. For it is written: 'He will command his angels concerning you, and they will lift you up in their hands, so that you will not strike your foot against a stone' " (v. 6). This was an appeal for Jesus to prove to people how important He was. It would have accomplished a good result in a wrong way by revealing His identity as the Son of God in a spectacular, flashy manner. Jesus knew this was not the way to use God's power. It would have been presumptuous to take God's power for granted. Jesus' response included a quotation from Deuteronomy: "Do not test the Lord your God" (Deut. 6:16). Testing God is not the same as trusting Him. Testing Him is the sort of situation where a person might say, "Lord, please protect me while I go play on the freeway to show my friends how much you love me."

This temptation was an appeal to the ego—to induce Jesus to substitute His own plan for God's. But Jesus wouldn't have anything to do with that. He knew that God's plans are the best. He chose to do what God told Him to do. This is the second key that unlocks the chains of temptation: to do what God tells us to do. Listening to God is the first step, doing what He says is the second step in resisting temptation.

Answer Number Three: Center Your Life on God

The final temptation was Satan's suggestion that he would give Jesus all the kingdoms of the world if He would bow down and worship him (see Matt. 4:8,9). If Jesus had yielded, Satan promised He would gain great glory and all the kingdoms, without going to the cross. But it would have been wrong, because we are to worship God alone, and serve only Him. It doesn't matter how tough things get or what rewards are offered, we are to worship the only One who is worthy of our worship—the God of the universe. No mere created being, like Satan, merits our worship. Furthermore, if Jesus had worshiped Satan, and gained all the glory and kingdoms without going to the cross, all of us would still be in our sins and would not have the salvation that Jesus came to provide.

Jesus knew all this, and so He responded once again by quoting appropriate Scripture and by resisting Satan: "Away from me, Satan! For it is written: 'Worship the Lord your God, and serve him only' " (v. 10).

Students need to understand that there is nothing wrong with wanting and having nice things—but it becomes wrong if we go about it in the wrong way. If we lie, cheat, steal, covet, step on others, worship false gods, or make gaining things more important than obeying God, our pursuit of possessions is sinful.

Junior highers are very possession-oriented. They go after money and what it can buy—and the things they want are often quite expensive. Their temptations in this area include coveting and stealing.

In this struggle with Satan, Jesus faced temptations of the same kind we face every day. In His final response to the Devil, Christ made it clear that He was dedicated to worshiping and serving only the Father. This is the third key that unlocks the chain of temptation: center our lives on God.

If we do these three things: listen to God, do what He says, and stay glued to Him, Satan will have a very tough time finding room to enter in.

Junior high students can do these three things. They can get to know the Bible. They can do what it says. And they can decide to live for the Lord, to say no to temptation.

SESSION PLAN

BEFORE CLASS BEGINS: Obtain the materials described in the EXPLORATION. Prepare your classroom as described in the ATTENTION GRABBER and in Step 4 of the EXPLORATION. Also, if you plan to do the OPTION, you will need at least one wooden measuring stick.

Attention Grabber

ATTENTION GRABBER (5-10 minutes)

Before class begins, attach a large sheet of butcher paper to the wall. As students arrive, provide several felt pens and explain, **You're going to write some graffiti expressing different temptations that face Christian junior high kids today. You've probably seen graffiti on walls of buildings—now's your chance to do some without being arrested! Write your comments about temptation on the large sheet of paper.**

After all students have arrived and have had time to write, read several of the graffiti. If you have thought of a temptation the students have missed,

write it on the paper. Make a transition to the EXPLORATION by saying, **Everyone faces temptation. Even our Lord Jesus Christ had some tough temptations to deal with.** Ask a good reader to read Hebrews 4:15. Point out that one important purpose of a high priest was to take care of the sins of the people. Say, **Jesus is the final high priest because, though He experienced the same sort of temptations we do, He did not sin. Today we are going to find out how He handled the problem of temptation.**

[handwritten note: unclear?]

[handwritten note: —really need to have examples here.]

Bible Exploration

EXPLORATION (35-50 minutes)

Materials needed: For Step 4 you will need a painter's drop cloth, the kind that is paper on one side and plastic on the other. You will also need

spray paint. If you like, obtain spray adhesive and glitter, paintbrushes, paint, and necessary clean-up items such as paper towels.

If you choose to do the CREATIVE OPTION, you will need at least one wooden yardstick or a similarly shaped piece of wood.

Step 1 (5-8 minutes): If you have six or more students, assemble them into three groups. (Otherwise, stay in one group.) Assign each group an identification: *A, B,* or *C.* Distribute copies of The Compass, one to each student.

Read Mark 1:12,13 to your class, and tell them that you want them to turn to the fourth chapter of Matthew to see in greater detail what sort of temptation Jesus faced. Have someone in Group A read Matthew 4:1-4 loud enough for all to hear. Then ask a member of Group B to read verses 5-7. Finally, someone from Group C should read verses 8-11.

Now look at your student worksheets. I want each group to work the proper portions of the assignment under Part 1. Do not do Part 2 yet. Answer each question as best you can, and I will walk around and help you if you have questions. When you have finished, each group will report to the entire class what has been learned. You've got five minutes.

Step 2 (10-12 minutes): When groups are through, have someone from each group sum up what they have found. Lead a discussion based on students' findings and comments. As you cover "How Did Jesus Respond?" (the last column on the worksheet), write on the chalkboard the three answers from the INSIGHTS FOR THE LEADER: Listen to God; do what He says; and center your life on Him.

Say something like, **These are the three things that you and I as Christians can do to conquer temptation. If we are in the habit of reading the Bible, doing what it says, and sticking close to God, we will find that many of those temptations just don't come around any more.**

CREATIVE OPTION (3 minutes)

Materials needed: At least one measuring stick or a similar piece of wood, and three sheets of newsprint or butcher paper, each about 11X17 inches.

NOTE: We strongly urge you to practice this demonstration at home with another yardstick, to be sure you know how to set it up properly.

As students watch, label the sheets with the three answers Jesus gave Satan, one answer per sheet. Put the wooden measuring stick on the surface of a table and hit it with your fist as shown:

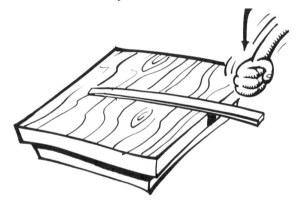

The stick will fly off the table. Now put the stick back as before, but cover it with the three sheets of paper as shown:

When you hit the end of the stick, it will break. The weight of the paper (and the air above it) is sufficient to make the stick immovable.

Tell your students, **Even though these three sheets of paper and the answers they contain seem lightweight or unimportant, together they can defeat the strongest fist. In the same way, a person who practices these three things will be able to stand up to temptation.**

Step 3 (10-12 minutes): Take the graffiti poster off the wall and use a pair of scissors to cut out and distribute the graffiti (several to each group). Instruct students to use their graffiti as they respond to Part 2 of the worksheet.

When students have finished, lead a short discussion to see that they clearly understand the concepts they have been dealing with.

Step 4 (10-15 minutes): If time is short, skip ahead to the CONCLUSION.

Before class begins, hang the drop cloth on one wall of your classroom, paper side out, plastic side against the wall. Students will paint on the paper and the plastic will prevent soak-through. Some drop cloths are brown, which is fine for use here.

Tell students, **In Jesus' day, Satan was often called Beelzebub, an insult which literally translated means "lord of flies." Now we are going to use these cans of spray paint to make a great work of art: a giant flyswatter!**

Have students gather around the drop cloth. Distribute the spray cans (after suitable words of warning) and instruct students to make a large flyswatter labeled with the three answers Jesus gave Satan (which should still be written on your chalkboard). Have some kids paint "flies" which represent various temptations. Allow students to stand on chairs when necessary. Encourage your learners to have a lot of fun and not worry too much about creating a masterpiece. If you like, allow students to use spray glue and glitter, paintbrushes, felt markers or any other means to add the finishing touches to the artwork.

When time is up, have students quickly clean up and return to their seats.

Conclusion and Decision

CONCLUSION (3-5 minutes)

Say, **I want you each to draw a small flyswatter on a piece of blank paper. Label it with the three things a Christian can do to be strong against temptation. Then draw or write a temptation you've been struggling with. Prayerfully ask God to help you win the victory over this temptation. Fold the flyswatter into your Bible and keep it as a reminder of what you have learned today.**

Close in prayer and distribute the Fun Page as students leave.

Note: For Session 3 you will need several broken items. A broken camera, tool, and small appliance will do nicely. See page 41 for details.

COMPASS

N
W E
S

PART 1: JESUS' TEMPTATIONS

Satan tempted Jesus to do what?	What would Jesus gain (what did Satan promise)?	Why would it be wrong?	How did Jesus respond?

▸**Group A**
  Read
  Matthew 4:1-4

▸**Group B**
  Read
  Matthew 4:5-7

▸**Group C**
  Read
  Matthew 4:8-11

PART 2: PEOPLE TODAY

			What would be a good response?

Using the graffiti you have been given, fill in the columns as they relate to a person your age.

Session 2

ARROWS AND ANSWERS!

Start Star: ☆

Satan tempts everybody, including YOU! Here's a game that will help you remember three important ways to defeat temptation and walk away clean. Here's how to play:

1. Put your pencil point on the star, close your eyes and try to draw a line to the Move Indicator. Open your eyes.

2. Now put your pencil point on the large dot in the center of the game board. Draw a line the proper distance and direction as indicated by your line on the Move Indicator. (An example has been done for you.)

3. As you continue to do 1 and 2, your line will wander across the game board. When you land on an arrow, you are wounded by a temptation. Three arrows and you lose. But when you land on any Bible, you defeat one arrow. You must get at least one each of Bibles 1, 2 and 3 in order to win. If your path runs into the outer wall, put your pencil back on the Start Dot.

Move Indicator:

Go 1 dot north	Go 2 dots east
Go 2 dots south	Go 1 dot west
Go 1 dot east	Go 2 dots north
Go 2 dots west	Go 1 dot south

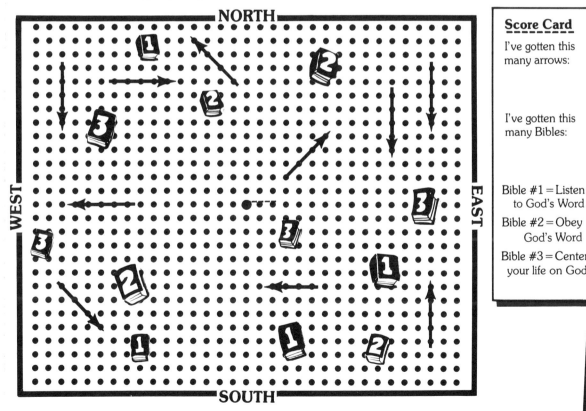

NORTH

WEST / **EAST**

SOUTH

Score Card

I've gotten this many arrows:

I've gotten this many Bibles:

Bible #1 = Listen to God's Word

Bible #2 = Obey God's Word

Bible #3 = Center your life on God

DAILY NUGGETS

Day 1 Read Mark 1:9-13. Who attended Jesus when He resisted Satan?

Day 2 Mark 1:21-28. Why did it bother the evil spirit that Jesus was holy?

Day 3 Mark 1:32-35. Why did the people seek Jesus? Why do you suppose Jesus sought His Father in prayer?

Day 4 Mark 2:1-12. Why did Jesus forgiving sins upset the teachers?

Day 5 Mark 2:13-17. Why did Jesus eat with sinners?

Day 6 Mark 3:7-12. When unclean spirits saw Jesus, what happened? What did Jesus say?

"For we do not have a high priest who is unable to sympathize with our weaknesses, but we have one who has been tempted in every way, just as we are—yet was without sin."

Hebrews 4:15

Listen to God! Do what He says! Stick close to Him! If you do, temptation won't be a major problem for you.

THEME: Trials and Temptations

Session 2

BIBLE STUDY OUTLINE

Read James 1:1-15 to your students. Make these points as time allows:

- James, the author, was probably Jesus' brother. The letter was written to people who had been scattered by persecution for their faith.
- In this part of the book, James stresses that Christians face two kinds of problems: trials which come from the outside, and temptations to sin which come from the inside.
- In verse 2, we are told to "Consider it pure joy" when trials come. Trials can come in many forms. They can be financial problems, they can be physical disabilities or illness, they can even be rejection by friends for our faith in God. Some of you may have been scorned by friends because you refused to do something morally wrong. Whatever the case, the Bible says we should accept the trial with a sense of joy. Why? Because trials cause us to become better people in the long run.
- First of all, in verse 3, we see that trials must be faced with faith. Nothing builds faith like a situation we can't handle! And faith that is stretched and tested develops perseverance, which means "stick-to-itiveness." And that's a real mark of a strong Christian, one who won't fade away when things are tough. This is a mature and complete Christian.
- Wisdom—not head knowledge, but spiritual insight into why things are as they are—will enable you to face trials with joy. This wisdom comes from God (v. 5).
- In verses 9-11, we see that poverty was a trial that many Christians apparently faced. The rich weren't safe from trials, either. No matter who you are, trials come. Be prepared by living with faith in God.
- In verse 13, we see the other side of the coin; the sin temptations that come from within. God allows trials so that we may grow and mature, but He doesn't bring temptations, for they are designed to make us fail and to sin. [At this point, begin the OBJECT LESSON.]
- Verses 14 and 15 show the natural progression of sin: temptation, desire, sin, and death. This is exactly the way Eve sinned—first the serpent tempted her to eat the forbidden fruit, then she saw that the fruit was desirable, then she took and ate it (see Genesis 3:1-6). Because of this, all of humanity has been under the curse of spiritual death. Only Jesus can save us from that death.
- There is nothing wrong with temptation, but when you desire to give in, you sin. The key to avoiding sin is to avoid temptation. There are two important parts to avoiding temptation. One is the spiritual part of running away from temptation by always running to God. Center your life on Him, listen to Him and do what He says. If you make this a habit, you will find that many things that used to tempt you no longer seem important. The second part is the practical thing of just staying away from things that tempt you. If you are tempted to drink at drinking parties, then stay away from those parties!

OBJECT LESSON: THE SIN TRAP

As you speak about sin, show your listeners various traps, such as a mousetrap, "roach motel," gopher trap or poison, a cage, rope to represent a snare, and a shovel or trowel to represent the pit of sin. Explain to students that sins—even seemingly "harmless" ones—are traps that will cause us great problems in life. Spend a moment on the forgiveness available to believers.

DISCUSSION QUESTIONS

1. **Why doesn't God just stop all problems when a person becomes a Christian?**
2. **What are some typical problems and temptations that Christians your age face?**
3. **Why is a doubter like a wave (James 1:6-8)? How do you suppose a person can stop being unstable and double-minded?**
4. **Who has God promised the crown of life to (v.12)? What kind of life and death (v. 15) is James talking about?**
5. **How can we be sure we have this life?**
6. **What are the things we should be doing to center our lives on God?**

THE COMPLETE JUNIOR HIGH
BIBLE STUDY RESOURCE
BOOK #2

These games may cause a few trials.

MARSHMALLOW DODGEBALL

Players all line up against the wall, except one who stands behind the foul line as illustrated. The foul line (which can be a rope or a piece of tape) is about twelve feet from the wall. The single player uses a slingshot to fire a marshmallow at the crowd. If someone is hit, that player replaces the original player. The original player goes out of the game. Play continues until only one "target" remains—that person is the winner.

TOE-TO-TOE

Two players attempt to hit each other with a paddle ball, without being hit. Players stand on marks about six feet apart. Players may not leave the marks, but they may try to duck and dodge. Because one player will probably be hit quickly, make it the best two out of three or three out of five per round. Always make the players wear eye protection. Winners can play winners to find the ultimate champion.

TABLETOP ICE HOCKEY

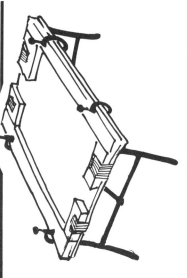

You can create a pretty good poor man's version of one of those tabletop air hockey games by using a smooth wooden or laminate table ringed with two-by-fours as shown. Use duck tape or C-clamps to secure the wood. An ice cube serves as the puck and any suitable object such as a plastic tumbler will do as a hockey stick (the heavier the "stick," the better). This game will also work very well on a tile floor. The ice cube won't bounce off the table as easily as a small ball.

Lord Over Demons and Diseases

Evil, Power, Trouble.

INSIGHTS FOR THE LEADER

WHAT THE SESSION IS ABOUT

Jesus has authority over evil spirits and diseases.

SCRIPTURE STUDIED

Mark 1:23-28,30-34,40-45; 5:1-20; 7:24-30.

KEY PASSAGE

"On hearing this, Jesus said to them, 'It is not the healthy who need a doctor, but the sick. I have not come to call the righteous, but sinners.' "
Mark 2:17

AIMS OF THE SESSION

During this session your learners will:

1. Examine some accounts of Jesus' power over demons and diseases.
2. Create a "newspaper" based on one of these accounts.
3. Plan a way to communicate, through practical actions, Christ's care for the hurting.

The topic of this session is Jesus' power over demons and diseases, His ability to help and heal people no matter what their problems. Your students may show a particular interest in the subject of the occult or demon possession. Since the main point of this session is to focus on Jesus and His power, rather than demons, avoid getting sidetracked. However, if there is strong interest, consider holding a special meeting to give junior highers an opportunity to have their questions answered.

The Scriptures your class will examine during the EXPLORATION portion of the session plan show three incidents of Jesus casting out demons and two cases of His healing physical disease.

The Holy One of God

The first miracle recorded in Mark is the deliverance of a man possessed by an evil spirit (see Mark 1:23-28). Jesus was teaching in a synagogue, and people were amazed at His authority. The spirit recognized Jesus and His mission, and cried out, "What do you want with us, Jesus of Nazareth? Have you come to destroy us? I know who you are—the Holy One of God!" (v. 24). Jesus made the spirit leave the man and the people were amazed again. They said, "What is this? A new teaching—and with authority! He even gives orders to evil spirits and they obey him" (v. 27). And the news about Jesus spread quickly.

Jesus' ability to cast out the demon shows that He has authority and power in the spiritual realm. It also shows His love for people. He cared about the man who was suffering from the evil spirits, and He cares about people's hurts today, whether these are spiritual, physical, emotional, or any other kinds of hurts.

Legion

The next incident your students will examine is the deliverance of the man possessed by "Legion"—a great many demons (see Mark 5:1-20). These demons were causing the man to live among tombs and to suffer such torment that he cried out day and night and cut himself with stones. People in the area had tried to chain him, but he broke the chains.

It is interesting to observe the apparent struggle between the man and the evil spirits. The man tried to tell his name, but the spirits intervened with their, "Legion." The spirits begged to be allowed to go into the pigs. Jesus gave them permission to do so. After the evil spirits went into the pigs, the entire herd of about 2,000 pigs rushed down the steep bank and drowned in the lake.

When the local people found out about the man's deliverance and the destruction of the pigs, they asked Jesus to leave the area. Evidently this demonstration of His divine authority frightened them. The man who had been demon possessed wanted to go with Jesus, but

NOTES

the Lord gave him a different job to do. He told him, "Go home to your family and tell them how much the Lord has done for you, and how he has had mercy on you" (v. 19). So the man did as he was told, and everyone was amazed. When Jesus helps people, He wants them in turn to help others.

The Woman's Daughter

The final example of Jesus' power over demons that will be examined in this session is the deliverance of the daughter of the Syrophoenician woman (see Mark 7:24-30). Jesus' conversation with the mother may be difficult for junior high students to understand, for it sounds as though Jesus is being harsh. Point out that Jesus was probably testing her faith, giving her an opportunity to show Him how much she really believed in Him. We need to see the glint of warmth and humor beneath the words both of Jesus and the woman. And, of course, in the end He did cast the spirit out of the woman's daughter.

Peter's Mother-in-law

During the session your learners will also look at the healing of Peter's mother-in-law (recorded in Mark 1:30,31). She was in bed with a fever; He "took her hand and helped her up. The fever left her and she began to wait on them" (v. 31). Later that evening Jesus healed many people with various diseases and cast out many demons. His power was becoming known, and people who needed help flocked to Him.

The Man with Leprosy

Finally your students will explore the healing of the man with leprosy (see Mark 1:40-45). The interaction between the man and Jesus is worth noting. The man said, "If you are willing, you can make me clean" (v. 40). Jesus' response showed how much He cared about people. "Filled with compassion, Jesus reached out His hand and touched the man. 'I am willing,' he said. 'Be clean!' Immediately the leprosy left him and he was cured" (vv. 41,42).

Make sure your students understand the significance of the fact that Jesus touched the man. In that day, no one wanted to touch a person with leprosy. Even a person's family wouldn't touch him, for fear of getting this terrible disease. Yet Jesus touched this man—probably the first human touch he had had in years. Jesus not only healed the disease, He reached out to the man's hurting heart by giving him that touch.

The incidents examined in this lesson are just a small sample of the many instances of healing found in the New Testament. Jesus healed and delivered many, many people, showing the power and authority He has over all of life's problems. His miracles were the proof to many people that His teachings were true. Jesus loved people and wanted to help them with all their hurts. He offers His help and love to your students today. And He also wants them to be part of His ministry of loving and helping others.

SESSION PLAN

BEFORE CLASS BEGINS: Obtain the materials listed in the ATTENTION GRABBER and the EXPLORATION.

Attention Grabber

ATTENTION GRABBER (2-3 minutes)

Materials needed: A few broken objects such as a camera, hand tools, small appliances and plates.

After students have sat down, reveal the broken objects to them. Say, **These objects are not quite whole. They are damaged goods, not in the shape they should be in. If they had personalities, I'm sure they would be unhappy.**

Now I want to ask you a question. When something breaks, who knows best how to fix it? Help students see that the person who made each object is the one best able to fix it.

Make a transition to the EXPLORATION by saying something like this: **Some people's lives have been broken by sickness, Satan, or sin. Jesus, who is our Creator, is totally qualified to mend broken and hurting people. Today we will take a look at some ways Jesus touched hurting people.**

[handwritten margin notes: — wrong choices — carefully! — Evil, — family hurts? — together — dies — no live — friends move away —]

Bible Exploration

EXPLORATION (30-50 minutes)

Materials needed: Large sheets of paper, felt markers, scissors and rubber cement.

Step 1 (10-12 minutes): Tell students, **You are about to become reporters. Newspaper reporters. You are going to research some incidents in the life of Christ and then, working together, you will create a newspaper that reports the facts you learn. The newspaper will contain news articles, editorials, cartoons, headlines, an advice column or two, even advertisements. I'll give you felt markers for the headlines, glue and scissors in a minute. But first, complete your research by doing the assignment on your Compass worksheets.**

Assemble students into small groups and give

Your students may wish to see this solution to the Fun Page puzzle.

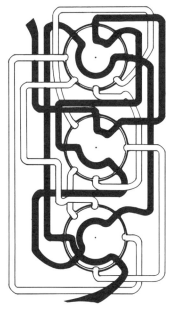

Note: Session 4 has several fun games for your students to play. Be sure you read and understand the rules to the games so that you can help students who may have questions. The games require tokens and other easy-to-find items. See page 50 for details.

each student a copy of the worksheet. Assign each group one or two of the Scripture passages to research. If your class is small, have each individual work alone.

When groups have finished, lead a quick discussion of what each learned. Have all students fill in their worksheets as the discussion progresses.

Step 2 (15-25 minutes): Now say, **It's time to start "putting our paper to bed," as they say in the news business. But first, we have to give it a name. What shall we call our paper?** Allow students to volunteer some fun titles. Have a vote for the winning name.

Now allow each group to pick one or more of the incidents. Or you may wish to assign topics. Say, **OK, you now have your topics. I want the people in each group to write articles, draw cartoons or "photographs," do sports reports, editorials, advice for the lovelorn columns, or anything else you can think of so that we can put together a truly great paper.**

Make sure you are accurate about the essential points of the story you are covering. However, use your imagination to add believable details of things that might have happened. Use the materials provided to create your articles, cartoons, and so on.

Instruct your "reporters" to write on small sheets of paper which they can later glue to one big sheet. As groups work, walk around and encourage students to let their creative juices flow.

Step 3 (5-10 minutes): Place large sheets of paper on a table or a clear space on the floor and allow all the students to assemble their articles into a big newspaper using scissors, glue and large sheets of paper. When students have finished, allow them to tape or tack their paper to the wall or bulletin board.

Step 4 (2-3 minutes): Have students return to their seats. Make a transition to the CONCLUSION by saying something like this: **We have reported on some ways Jesus touched the lives and met the needs of some hurting people. There are still people in need today, even here in our church family. Some are lonely, some troubled by the problems of old age. Many have troubles at home or at school. Some have problems with self-image, or with financial concerns. Jesus still helps these people, and often He uses people like you and me to do it.**

Conclusion and Decision

CONCLUSION (5 minutes)

Direct students to the "Who's Hurting?" section of The Compass and explain, **You are to fill in the initials of someone you know who is hurting physically, emotionally, or spiritually. Think about the example of Jesus and the fact that you are God's child. Then decide one practical thing that you could do for the person you are thinking of. You might pray for the person, or write a note, take a flower or send a gift. Whatever you write, make it something specific and something you yourself could do.**

(If you have students you know are not believers, or anyone who is hurting too much to help, be sure to mention that anyone in such a state can come to Jesus for help and healing.)

When time is up, lead the class in silent prayer, asking each student to pray for the person he or she has selected.

Distribute the Fun Page.

Check It Out!

You are a reporter covering Jesus Christ. Your "Managing Editor" has assigned you one or more of the following Bible passages to cover. Read the passage, and describe what happened in one or two sentences.

Mark 1:23-28

Mark 5:1-20

Mark 7:24-30

Mark 1:30-34

Mark 1:40-45

▷ ▷ ▷ ▷ ▷ ▷ ▷ ▷ ▷ ▷ ▷ Who's Hurting? ▷ ▷ ▷
▷ ▷ ▷

Perhaps you know someone who is having physical, emotional, or spiritual problems. Write his or her initials here: _____

Just as Jesus helped those who were in need, you can do something, too! Think for a moment and write one practical thing you could do for the person listed above. (Having problems thinking of something? Here's a hint: Prayer, share, and care.)

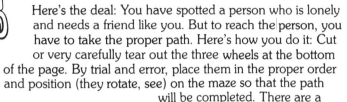

HELP ME, ALREADY!

If you've never tried one of our famous "shuffle the pieces" mazes, hoo-boy, are you in for a shock! These things can take *all day* to solve.

Here's the deal: You have spotted a person who is lonely and needs a friend like you. But to reach the person, you have to take the proper path. Here's how you do it: Cut or very carefully tear out the three wheels at the bottom of the page. By trial and error, place them in the proper order and position (they rotate, see) on the maze so that the path will be completed. There are a couple of rules: The path you draw with your pencil must go through each circle **twice.** And you cannot move any wheel once you begin a new path. An example of a wrong guess is shown. Your teacher has the solution.

SNIFF!

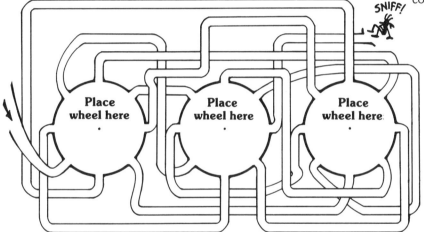

Place wheel here   **Place wheel here**   **Place wheel here**

Typical wrong solution:

P.S. There are over 3000 possible combinations! Try pinning the wheels with thumbtacks to make things a little easier.

How well have you done? No, not at playing the maze—how well have you done at being a friend? Just as Jesus came to heal and help people in need, you too can show Christian love to others. Be a friend, not just to your good pals, but to people who really need to find a friend.

DAILY NUGGETS

Day 1 Read Mark 3:14,15. What job did Jesus give the twelve disciples? How would you feel if you had been one of the twelve?

Day 2 Mark 3:22-27. In your own words, how did Jesus respond to the charge that He was possessed by Beelzebub?

Day 3 Mark 3:28-30. What is the one sin that will never be forgiven?

Day 4 Mark 3:31-35. Who are Jesus mother and brothers? Are you a member of His family?

Day 5 Mark 4:21-23. What is the purpose of a lamp? How can Christians be "lamps" for the Lord?

Day 6 Mark 4:24,25. Would you like to be treated as you treat others? Are there some changes you need to make in your actions?

"On hearing this, Jesus said to them, 'It is not the healthy who need a doctor, but the sick. I have not come to call the righteous, but sinners.'"

Mark 2:17

Session 3

THEME: Jesus can work miracles.

BIBLE STUDY OUTLINE

This study is based on John 9. As time allows, make these points:

- Verses 1-3: In Jesus' day, the rabbis (religious teachers) taught that all suffering was punishment for sin. They even believed that a baby could sin while in its mother's womb! Also, they felt that children could be punished for sins of the parents. In verse 3, Jesus contradicted these teachings. Sin can cause troubles, but not all troubles are caused by sins. Sometimes, as it says in the first chapter of James, trials come to help us grow spiritually.

- Verses 6,7: Wow! What a strange way to heal a person! But Christ never was conventional; when He said or did anything, people either responded with love and joy or with hate and rejection. We see the same thing today: Some people love our Lord, some people don't. There is no room for the middle-of-the road attitude. You are either living for Him, or against Him.

- Verses 8-34: Jesus' miracle caused a huge controversy in the neighborhood. When God works, people react—not always positively. You may have seen this in your own Christian life. Some of you may have parents who aren't happy about your commitment to God. Some of your friends may be afraid to become Christians because they value their sins too much. They know God will change them. The controversy over the cured man ended with his being thrown out of the synagogue (excommunicated).

- Verses 35-38: Jesus found the man later, and the man worshiped Him, something that is proper to do only to God. Notice the progression of this man's belief in Christ: First, he calls Him a man (v. 11); then a prophet (v. 17); then a man from God (v. 33); and finally he worships Him as God (v. 38). Getting to know about Christ is a progressive thing. If this is the first Bible study you've ever been to, this may be the first time you've seen Christ in a positive light. As you experience Him more and more, you may eventually come to realize He is Lord and Master. You can become a Christian at any time, of course, but as you spend time with Christ, you will appreciate who He is more and more.

- Verses 39-41: This part may have happened a bit later. The Pharisees are now with Jesus. He uses the opportunity to point out that people who think they don't need Him are the blindest people of all. The blind man who was cured also gained spiritual sight: he recognized who Jesus was. The Pharisees were blind to this truth. Do you recognize who Jesus is? If not, you are blind.

TRUE STORY: A MIRACLE

Tell of a miracle you have experienced, or of one you have heard about. Or tell the following true story.

Ernie was a high school kid who had just become a Christian. At first, Ernie didn't realize it was wrong for a Christian to smoke marijuana. As soon as he found out, he quit.

But it wasn't long before he gave in to temptation. After having a smoke, he went for a ride on his bike, his conscience bothering him. Suddenly Ernie was hit by a car. He flew off his bike, flew over the car and landed on his feet on the concrete. He was completely unhurt!

Ernie knew it was a miracle—God's way of saying, "Watch out, Ernie, you're playing with fire." So Ernie vowed never to smoke pot again.

But he did. And believe it or not, he fell off a cliff! This time Ernie was hurt. He broke his knee cap. He apologized to God for his sin, and vowed never to do it again. While attending a church service with Ernie, a friend of his prayed that the knee would be healed. At that very moment, Ernie said, "My knee! It feels OK!" Ernie removed his cast and, sure enough, the doctors could find nothing wrong. The amazing thing is, Ernie did not know his friend had prayed for him.

Ernie vowed he would never smoke again and, after two miracles, he never did.

DISCUSSION QUESTIONS

1. **We have said that a person is either for Jesus or against Him, that there is no real middle-of-the-road attitude. Why not?**
2. **Have you known anyone who said, "I know Jesus is real, but I'm not ready to become a Christian"? What are some of the reasons a person might say this, and why is it a foolish thing to say?**
3. **Jesus said, "As long as it is day, we must do the work of him who sent me" (v. 4). Does the word "we" include you and me today? What sort of work do you think God wants us to do?**

THE COMPLETE JUNIOR HIGH
BIBLE STUDY RESOURCE
BOOK #2

Fun with food.

WASTE 'EM WITH WATERMELONS

After you have your standard watermelon eating contest, try a couple of seed spitting competitions:

1. Spit for distance, appointing one person to measure with a tape, and three judges to award points for "form, grace, and style."

2. Spit for accuracy. Place cups on the ground or on a table as shown. Label cups with point values.

BANANA/7-UP CONTEST

This is one of the all-time crack-up games. Players each eat a banana as fast as possible, then immediately down a 7-up. The results can be messy.

BOBBING FOR AVOCADOS

The above game has been around since the sixties, at least. This one is a newer version of the very old apple bobbing game. Peel avocados and put them in the water instead of apples. Fun!

His Power

INSIGHTS FOR THE LEADER

WHAT THE SESSION IS ABOUT

The power of Jesus over nature.

SCRIPTURE STUDIED

Mark 4:35-41; 5:22-24,35-43; 6:32-53.

KEY PASSAGE

"Take courage! It is I. Don't be afraid." Mark 6:50b

AIMS OF THE SESSION

During this session your learners will:

1. Review four miracles of Christ by playing four games.
2. Discuss the power of Christ.
3. Prayerfully ask God to miraculously help them in a specific area of need.

This session is a very special change of pace from our normal lessons. Your students will spend almost the entire class time playing four fun games based on four miracles of Christ. But the purpose of the games is not just to have fun! To play and win these games, your students must read and understand in great detail the assigned Scriptures.

Jesus Calms the Storm

Jesus' miracles validate His claims He made about Himself which students examined in the first session. He knew that people had to have more than just His word for it that He is the Son of God and is able to provide forgiveness, a new life and so on. Therefore, He demonstrated His supernatural abilities. Since He is the Creator, Jesus is able to use, to suspend, or to transcend the laws of nature which He created.

The first passage you and your students will study is Mark 4:35-41, the record of Jesus calming the storm. As you can read in the passage, Jesus was asleep in the boat—probably a sign that He was exhausted after a busy day of serving the Father by ministering to people. Junior high leaders often have the same experience!

The Sea of Galilee is subject to sudden, violent wind storms, but this storm was unusually strong. The disciples were so frightened that they woke Jesus up. He spoke to the

storm and it immediately calmed down. The words He spoke to the storm include a term that literally means "be muzzled."

Jesus Gives Life

While the last session examined two incidents of healing, the extension of this power to reverse the finality of death is awe inspiring, to say the least. Mark 5:22-24, 35-48 is the passage your learners will read—the recounting of Jesus raising a little girl back to life.

When Jesus spoke to the girl and took her hand, He reversed the natural process of decay that comes with death. He is the Creator and giver of life, and He gave it back to the little girl who had lost hers.

It is interesting to note Mark's inclusion of the Aramaic phrase *Talitha koum!* in this account written in Greek. Jesus obviously spoke to the girl in the language with which she was most familiar, evidence of His continuing pattern of reaching out to people in individual ways, touching lives in the most helpful ways possible.

Jesus Feeds Five Thousand

Mark 6:32-44 records the feeding of five thousand men. Jesus demonstrated once again His authority over the world of nature. He is the One who made the fish and who put the grain in the earth and caused it to multiply.

One of the intriguing aspects of this miracle

is the way in which Jesus involved His disciples in the process. As long as He was multiplying bread and fish, it would have been no more difficult to have it magically appear in everybody's lap. However, He chose to involve His disciples in the distribution of the food. Again we see Jesus' great power mixed with human limitations, indicating His desire to have us be willing to let Him work through us.

Jesus Walks on Water

Later that same night the disciples were struggling against the wind as they sailed again across the lake. Jesus came to them, walking on the water! (See Mark 6:45-53.) Here the Creator transcended the law of gravity or the molecular structure of matter in order to accomplish this supernatural deed. Once again, He demonstrated His power and authority as God. In addition, the wind stopped after He got into the boat. This must have reminded the disciples of that earlier incident in which He calmed the storm.

It is important to be assured that the stories of Jesus' miracles are true, for these supernatural deeds demonstrate the validity of His claims about Himself. He claims to be God, the creator of the universe, and He showed His ability to control what He created. He demonstrated this authority in a number of ways: by calming a storm He showed His power over the natural elements; by raising the girl He showed His power over the forces of death and decay that had crept into His creation; by feeding the five thousand, and by walking on the water He demonstrated His authority over the laws of nature on which the whole of creation rests.

He is God, and by acknowledging His identity, trusting Him, and yielding to His control, your junior highers will find Him at work in their lives just as He worked in the lives of people among whom He lived on earth.

SESSION PLAN

BEFORE CLASS BEGINS: Familiarize yourself with each of the four games by reading the instructions and playing each one. Make the required photocopies (see below) and set up your classroom so that students have areas to play the games. Each game can be played by two, three, or four players. We recommend four when possible. Now read the CLASS-TIME INSTRUCTIONS to be sure you understand what to expect.

PHOTOCOPY INFORMATION

Because Game 1 is defaced when it is played, you will need at least four copies of it. Games 2,3, and 4 do not need to be photocopied unless you have more than 16 students. (There are four games. Up to four students can play the games. If you have more than 16 students, make copies of each game so that two or more groups can play the same game at the same time.)

CLASS-TIME INSTRUCTIONS

Step 1 (10-12 minutes): When students have arrived, assemble them into groups of four people each. (The last group formed must have at least two people. If you have only one, recruit a student from another group to join him or her.) Distribute the games, Game 1 to the first group, Game 2 to the second and so on. If you have more than four groups, two or more groups can be playing separate copies of the same game at the same time.

Explain, **Today we are going to have a lot of fun! I've handed out four different games to you, and if time allows each group will have a chance to play all four. Each game is about a miracle that Jesus performed. Read the instructions carefully and be sure to read the Bible verses that each game requires you to read. I'm going to give you about eight minutes to play each game. As you play, I'll come by to answer any questions you may have.**

Step 2 (variable time): When it seems as though most everyone has finished, have each group move to a new game for a second round. (If one or two groups finish well before the others, spend time discussing with them the nature of the games and what they learned about Jesus.) Do a third and fourth round as time allows.

Step 3 (10-12 minutes): Thank students for their cooperation. Collect all materials and have students sit down. Lead a discussion based on the following questions:

1. **We played four games today. What four miracles did we see Jesus perform? Describe them in detail.**
2. **What does the fact that Jesus could do these things tell us about Him?**
3. **Why is He able to control nature like this?**
4. **Is there anything that Jesus can't do?**
5. **Can He still do miracles today?**
6. **If Jesus can do all these things, do you think He is interested in working miracles in our lives—not just walking on water, but things like healing broken friendships or changing a hurting family situation or the like? Name some other things He can do for people like us.**

Step 4 (2-3 minutes): Conclude your class time by telling students to individually think of one area of their lives where they need God's miraculous help. To help them think, make a few suggestions of common needs such as grades in school, trouble with parents, loneliness, and so forth.

Close in prayer and distribute the Fun Page.

Note: Session 5 requires special materials. See the ATTENTION GRABBER and the EXPLORATION on page 69 for details.

Game 1   THE STORM! Mark 4:35-41

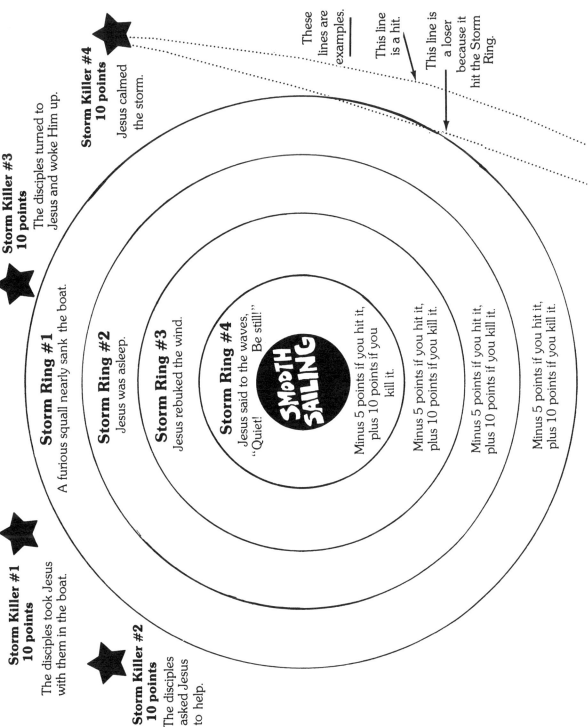

Storm Killer #3
10 points

The disciples turned to Jesus and woke Him up.

Storm Killer #4
10 points

Jesus calmed the storm.

Storm Killer #1
10 points

A furious squall nearly sank the boat.

Storm Ring #1
A furious squall nearly sank the boat.

Storm Ring #2
Jesus was asleep.

Storm Ring #3
Jesus rebuked the wind.

Storm Ring #4
Jesus said to the waves, "Quiet! Be still!"

SMOOTH SAILING

Storm Killer #2
10 points

The disciples asked Jesus to help.

The disciples took Jesus with them in the boat.

Minus 5 points if you hit it, plus 10 points if you kill it.

Minus 5 points if you hit it, plus 10 points if you kill it.

Minus 5 points if you hit it, plus 10 points if you kill it.

Minus 5 points if you hit it, plus 10 points if you kill it.

These lines are examples.

This line is a hit.

This line is a loser because it hit the Storm Ring.

Rockin' Boat

Instructions: Before you play this game, one player must read Mark 4:35-41 aloud. That player gets to take the first turn **and** earns 10 points! Here's how to play: The object of the game is to earn the most points before the game ends. The game ends when someone reaches the "Smooth Sailing" area by destroying all of the Storm Rings. To earn points, a player puts the point of his or her pencil on the "Rockin' Boat," closes his or her eyes (tight!) and attempts to draw a line to any one of the four Storm Killers at the top of the game. The player should not lift the pencil until after he or she says "Hit!" and then opens his or her eyes. If the pencil line ends on one of the Storm Killers, the player earns **10 points.** Lines that touch nothing or that pass **through and beyond** a Storm Killer are **minus 2 points.** If a line touches the outer Storm Ring, the player **loses 5 points.** DURING EACH TURN a player gets to try three lines, each starting at the Rockin' Boat. Storm Killers can be hit repeatedly, scoring points for the player each time.

A Storm Ring is eliminated when the Storm Killer with the same number as the Ring is first hit by a player's line. The player who eliminates the Ring gets **10 points** for hitting the Storm Killer and **10 points** for the Ring. When a Ring is eliminated, players can draw their lines across it with no penalty. As each outer Ring disappears, it will become easier to hit the Storm Killers. Make a pencil mark in each destroyed Ring as a reminder that it has been eliminated.

The game is over when all Rings are gone. However, it is the person with the MOST POINTS who wins, so players may want to rack up some extra points before they try to eliminate that last Ring!

Game 2
CAVES OF DEATH!
Mark 5:22-24, 35-43

Instructions: Before you play this game, one player must read Mark 5:22-24,35-43 aloud. It is the story of how Jesus saved a girl's life. The player who reads the passage gets to go first and take two turns in a row! Here's how to play: The object of the game is to be the first one to reach "Daylight!" at the top of the caves. Players take turns moving along the caves by spinning the paper clip spinner (as shown in the illustration) and jumping the number of spaces the spinner says. Each player needs a token to move, such as a coin or small shred of paper. When a player lands on a space with instructions, that player must READ THE INSTRUCTIONS ALOUD and do what it says. If you finish this game early, play it again.

Daylight!

Paper Clip Spinner

2 3 4 1 2 3 4 1

Put your pencil and a paper clip as shown. Spin the clip by hitting it with your finger.

You find flashlight. EXTRA TURN.

Cave bear attack! LOSE TURN.

You find water. JUMP UP ONE LEVEL.

Snake pit! LOSE TURN.

Vampire bats! DROP ONE LEVEL.

Jesus says, "Little girl, I say to you, get up!" JUMP AHEAD.

Find map. EXTRA TURN.

Cave-in. LOSE TURN.

The little girl stands and walks! YOU WIN!

Jesus says, "Don't be afraid; just believe." JUMP AHEAD

The daughter dies. DROP ONE LEVEL.

Darkness. GO BACK THREE.

Warm camp fire. AHEAD THREE.

Fresh air. AHEAD THREE.

Giant spiders! DROP ONE LEVEL.

Everyone laughs at Jesus. DROP ONE LEVEL.

Jesus leaves with Jairus to heal his daughter. JUMP WAY UP!

Lost in mystery caves. LOSE TURN.

Bigfoot! DROP ONE LEVEL.

Light up ahead! EXTRA TURN.

You recognize a landmark. AHEAD FOUR.

Cave men attack. FALL DOWN PIT.

Start

Game 3

Instructions to the Teacher: Cut out the individual cards and the box with the game instructions. (If more than one group will be playing this game at the same time, photocopy before cutting. IMPORTANT: If you make a photocopy, be sure the printing cannot be read through the back of the paper. If your photocopier can copy both sides, copy the pattern on the back of this page and the next. Otherwise, photocopy on cardstock or glue the cards to cardstock before cutting.)

CONCENTRATION CARD GAME! Mark 6:34-44

Instructions: Shuffle the cards and place them facedown as shown in the illustration. Before beginning play, one student must read Mark 6:34-44 aloud. LISTEN VERY CAREFULLY to the story or you won't play well!

Here's how to play: The first player turns up any two cards. If the cards match AND IF AND ONLY IF THE PLAYER CAN ANSWER THE QUESTION ON THE MATCHING CARDS he or she gets to collect the cards and take another turn. If the cards do NOT match or if the player CANNOT answer the question if they do match, the player must turn both cards facedown again. Then it is the next player's turn. The game is over when all cards have been collected. The player with the most cards wins.

IMPORTANT NOTE: Some of these questions are difficult. A player may not refer to the Bible while trying to guess an answer. But **after the guess has been made and the two cards turned back facedown, everyone should open the Bible and find the proper answer.** (The player whose turn it is next will probably be able to grab the two cards if he or she has been paying attention!) As the game progresses, players should memorize the answers to each question so they have a chance to win.

If you finish early, play again.

Jesus had compassion on the crowd because they were like what?	How many people were in the groups Jesus assembled?	In verse 34, Jesus taught the people what?
How many months' wages would it take to feed all the people?	Jesus looked at what before He gave thanks?	What two things did the disciples say to Jesus in verse 35?
How many loaves did they start with?	How many baskets full were collected?	In verse 37, Jesus told the disciples to do what?
How many fish did they start with?	How many men were in the crowd?	What did the crowd run on in verse 33?
Jesus had the people sit in groups on what?	In verse 32, how did Jesus and the disciples get to the solitary place?	What large thing did Jesus see in verse 34?

In verse 35, what part of the day was it?	Who picked up the baskets in verse 43?	Jesus had compassion on the crowd because they were like what?	How many people were in the groups Jesus assembled?	In verse 34, Jesus taught the people what?	In verse 35, what part of the day was it?	Who picked up the baskets in verse 43?
What did the disciples tell Jesus to do in verse 36?	Where did Jesus and the disciples go in verse 32?	How many months' wages would it take to feed all the people?	Jesus looked at what before He gave thanks?	What two things did the disciples say to Jesus in verse 35?	What did the disciples tell Jesus to do in verse 36?	Where did Jesus and the disciples go in verse 32?
Jesus gave thanks and then broke what in verse 41?	Who recognized Jesus and the disciples in verse 33?	How many loaves did they start with?	How many baskets full were collected?	In verse 37, Jesus told the disciples to do what?	Jesus gave thanks and then broke what in verse 41?	Who recognized Jesus and the disciples in verse 33?
What did Jesus give the disciples in verse 41?	What was surrounding the people in verse 36?	How many fish did they start with?	How many men were in the crowd?	What did the crowd run on in verse 33?	What did Jesus give the disciples in verse 41?	What was surrounding the people in verse 36?
In verse 42 the people _____ and were _____.	Jesus told the disciples to go and do what in verse 38?	Jesus had the people sit in groups on what?	In verse 32, how did Jesus and the disciples get to the solitary place?	What large thing did Jesus see in verse 34?	In verse 42 the people _____ and were _____.	Jesus told the disciples to go and do what in verse 38?

Game 4

Instructions to the Teacher: This game can be played two ways: either as a version of the old pitch penny game by placing it on the floor against the wall and letting students pitch pennies at it from about six feet away (the simplist way to play); or by assembling this game as shown and allowing students to play according to the instructions below. If you choose to do it the pitch penny way, cut both sets of instructions off the game and discard, then tell the students how to play. Either way, they must read the passage before they begin the game.

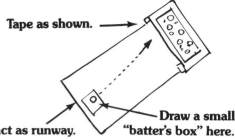

Tape as shown. ➝

➝ **Draw a small "batter's box" here.**

Sheet of 11x17-inches paper to act as runway.

Cut along this line before giving lower portion to students.

Instructions: Before beginning this game, one player must read Mark 6:45-53 aloud. The player who reads gets 10 points! The object of this game is to score the most points before the time is up. A player scores points by placing a penny in the little "batter's box" at the end of the sheet, and using another coin to bat the penny to one of the targets (see illustration). If a player's penny touches a target, he or she gets 10 points. If the penny hits one of the bad things, the player loses 5 points. A complete miss means no points are scored and the player must wait for his or her next turn.

Bat like this:

WALKING ON WATER! Mark 6:45-53

"Take courage! It is I."
10 POINTS

Shark

Jesus dismisses the crowd
10 POINTS

Whirlpool

Evening comes
10 POINTS

Disciples afraid of ghosts
10 POINTS

Crocodile

The wind dies down
10 POINTS

Jesus prays on the mountain
10 POINTS

Waterfall

Disciples see Jesus walking on the water
10 POINTS

Tidal wave

They land safely
10 POINTS

FUN Page!

Session 4

FIX IT!

"Then Jesus came to them and said, 'All authority in heaven and on earth has been given to me.'"
Matthew 28:18

Jesus walked on water to rescue His disciples. He cured the blind and lame. When something was terribly wrong, Jesus would put it RIGHT! Here's a picture with 24 things wrong with it. Let's see if YOU can put it right. Answers are at the bottom. Hey, don't look!

Answers: Man's upper lip is messed up, man has six fingers, his sunglasses are upside down, his earphones are plugged into the microphone jack, one musical note is upside down, cat has three ears, cat has knot in tail, man on television is reaching out, clock on wall has wrong number, wall calendar has 32 day month and six day weeks, shelf has one bracket upside down, cup on shelf has wrong liquid level, someone is hanging outside the window, window curtains are on the outside, chicken soap should be soup, soup can opened on bottom, vase contains longstem "noses," airplane's propeller has stopped, plane's wheels are square, clouds upside down, wall socket is wrong.

DAILY NUGGETS Wisdom from God's Word for you to read each day.

Day 1 Read Mark 4:37-41. Why were the disciples afraid, according to Jesus?

Day 2 Mark 5:1-20. In verse 19, what job did Jesus give the man? Has Jesus given you such a job?

Day 3 Mark 5:25-34. What caused Jesus to heal the woman? What did He say to her?

Day 4 Mark 5:21-24,35-43. What did Jesus say to Jairus? What did Jesus do?

Day 5 Mark 6:1-6. Why do you suppose the people had no faith in Jesus?

Day 6 Mark 6:7-12. What did the disciples preach? What does the word mean?

HOT-THOT

"Take courage! It is I. Don't be afraid."
Mark 6:50b

THE COMPLETE JUNIOR HIGH BIBLE STUDY RESOURCE BOOK #2
© 1987 GL/LIGHT FORCE, VENTURA, CA 93006

THEME: Disciples can have miraculous power.

Session 4

BIBLE STUDY OUTLINE

Read Acts 3:1-10, 4:4 to your listeners. As time allows, go over these points:

- Acts 3:1: Peter and John were two of Jesus' closest disciples. The word disciple means **learner** or **follower.** To be a disciple of Christ, you and I must commit ourselves to learning about Him and His teachings, and following Him all the time—by obeying Him. They were going to pray—to talk to their Lord. The key to remaining close to Jesus is to spend time talking to Him as well as reading His Word and obeying Him.
- Verses 2-5: The man had been crippled since birth, more than forty years (see 4:22). He obviously had little hope of ever being more than a beggar moved here and there by acquaintances.
- Verse 6: They had no money to give the man, but they had Jesus. And because they had Jesus, they had power. Notice that they said, "In the name of Jesus." This was not their power or authority, it was Jesus'. An important point here is that Jesus uses people who are close to Him. If you don't live for Him, you shouldn't expect to see Him use you in wonderful ways. In other words, you need to get close to Jesus as a disciple. When you are faithful to Him, He will work in and through you. Who knows—maybe He will call on you to heal someone, or lead a friend to Christ, or to be a youth pastor or missionary when you get older.
- Verses 7-10: The people were filled with wonder and amazement. When God works in someone's life, usually people begin to notice. It's hard not to notice when a stick of dynamite goes off. God's power can be that strong!
- Acts 4:4: Five thousand men believed because of the miracle and because of the message Peter preached. God's power was real in those days, just as it can be real in our lives now.

OBJECT LESSON: CRUTCHES

As you speak of the crippled man, show your listeners a crutch, old cast, or leg braces. Or teach from a wheelchair.

DISCUSSION QUESTIONS

1. **Is it possible to be an effective Christian without being a disciple? What exactly is a disciple? How does one become a disciple?**
2. **How often do you think we should pray? What does 1 Thessalonians 5:17 mean when it says to pray continually or without ceasing? John and Peter were going to the Temple for a formal time of prayer. Is there a difference between that kind of prayer and the kind 1 Thessalonians 5:17 is talking about?**
3. **Do you think there are less miracles today than in John and Peter's day? Why or why not?**
4. **Do you think miracles are reserved for a very few Christians each generation, or should we expect to see miracles in our own lives?**
5. **Is leading a friend to Christ any less a miracle than healing a crippled man?**

Teamwork in action.

BOAT RACES

Three players on each team carry a bench or board on their backs, doubled over as shown.

VARIATION: Players hold the bench or board as shown.

TABLE VOLLEYBALL

Team members must remain sitting as they toss the ball over the table "net" as in this illustration:

Standard volleyball rules apply.

FASHION POINTERS

Award points to people who are wearing certain items, and/or have certain items in their purses or wallets. Prepare a list of about 25 things, and keep track of players' point totals on a chalkboard or paper. Your list could contain things like: red shoes, white socks with blue stripes, a belt, a necklace, a ring, shirts with printed words or art, and so on.

The Four Soils

SESSION 5

INSIGHTS FOR THE LEADER

WHAT THE SESSION IS ABOUT

The parable of the four soils.

SCRIPTURE STUDIED

Mark 4:1-20.

KEY PASSAGE

"Others, like seed sown on good soil, hear the word, accept it, and produce a crop—thirty, sixty or even a hundred times what was sown."
Mark 4:20

AIMS OF THE SESSION

During this session your learners will:

1. Build a model landscape based on the four soils.
2. Compare the four soils to modern human nature.
3. Ask God to help them be examples of the good soil.

The Parable of the Sower

This parable is also rightly known as the parable of the four soils, for it is more about soils than it is about the sower or the seed; the sower remains the same, and so does the seed. Only the soils are different. The sower is anyone who preaches or teaches the Word. The seed is the Word of God. The different soils are representative of all who hear the gospel message. This is one of the few parables followed by a careful and detailed scriptural explanation.

The parable focuses on receptivity, the hearer's openness to receive the Word of God. The seed is sown generously, but much will be lost; many things may interfere with its growth. The sower has to have a great deal of patience and confidence.

This parable is saying that God, in His love, is willing to broadcast the seed, His Word, in every direction and into all kinds of soil with the knowledge that only some of the soils will receive the seed and bear fruit to His glory.

Paul says in 1 Corinthians 3:6,7, "I planted the seed, Apollos watered it, but God made it grow. So neither he who plants nor he who waters is anything, but only God, who makes things grow." It is God's good pleasure to make us grow. He wants us to receive His Word and multiply and mature in His love.

The first soil is the hardened path. In Palestine the parcels of land were divided not by fences but by paths, perhaps a foot or two wide. These paths were hardened by the steps of both people and animals and were sun-baked hard as pavement. When the seed fell onto these areas, it remained on the surface and would not germinate. It was walked on and eaten by birds.

The second soil was filled with rocks, and even though the seed took root, it withered from lack of access to moisture or deeper soil. Mark 4:5,6 says, "Some fell on rocky places, where it did not have much soil. It sprang up quickly, because the soil was shallow. But when the sun came up, the plants were scorched, and they withered because they had no root."

The third soil was rich but contaminated by thorn seeds, which are not noticeable in the beginning. After the good seed was sown, the thorns grew up to choke the life out of the plant so it could not bear fruit.

Finally, the fourth soil was the good soil that received the seed, and "produced a crop, multiplying thirty, sixty, or even a hundred times" (v. 8).

Verses 11 and 12 may elicit some questions from your students. Did Jesus not want the people to understand and be forgiven? The purpose of the parables was not only to enlighten those who would eventually understand, but also to expose the hardheartedness of many in the multitude.

NOTES

A Parable for Junior Highers

Jesus told the parable to a large crowd of people. Later, when He was alone with His disciples, He explained its meaning. In terms your young students will understand, the first soil (the hard-packed soil), is someone who is too busy for God, or who is turned off to God usually because he or she has not yet experienced the limitations of self-sufficiency and feels no need for God. This person says, "I want to do what I want to do. God would only get in my way."

The rocky soil represents someone who is enthusiastic about the gospel because his or her friends are becoming Christians or because of good-looking persons of the opposite sex at church, or because of an active youth program. This person recognizes that the gospel has something to offer, but he or she does not accept it personally. Such a person may be positive about the Christian faith, and may even declare its truth, but does not *possess* its truth. Persecution causes this person to fall away. For a junior high age person, "persecution" is anything that makes it uncomfortable to be a Christian. If a well-liked youth minister leaves, the faith of the "rocky soil" leaves, too. If his or her friends stop attending, this person soon quits too.

The thorny soil represents a person who decides to be friends with Jesus and follow Him. But he or she lets the affairs of the world take precedence. For a junior higher these may be sports activities, cheerleading, social groups, clubs. These activities are not bad in themselves, but they can take up so much energy and time that a junior higher has no time left for a personal relationship with God or for church, Sunday School, and youth group activities. Anything that crowds God out of one's life is a "thorn."

The good soil represents the young person who can grow unhindered in his or her relationship with Christ. This does not imply that the person is perfect, or has "arrived," but only that growth continues. The person keeps "short accounts" with God by confessing sins as soon as he or she becomes aware of them, and by taking problems to God instead of struggling with them alone. This junior high person is reading the Bible, praying, learning to obey God, attending church and youth group programs, loving others and so on. He or she is cooperating with God in order to become good soil.

This session should offer a challenge to your students to think about their receptivity to the Word of God. Christians are responsible to develop their responses to the Word so that God can bring a rich harvest of fruitfulness to their lives.

SESSION PLAN

BEFORE CLASS BEGINS: This session requires no Compass student worksheet or Teacher's Resource page, so there is no photocopying for this class, except the Fun Page. Both the ATTENTION GRABBER and the EXPLORATION call for special materials.

Attention Grabber

ATTENTION GRABBER (2-3 minutes)

Materials required: A box of detergent, a potted plant or a flower, a hand shovel and, if convenient, a copy of a magazine dedicated to the sport of dirt biking.

When students have arrived and are seated, tell them, **I'm going to show you several objects. I want you to put your heads together and think of one important thing all these objects have in common.**

Show the students the detergent and other objects. The answer you are looking for is "dirt." If necessary, you can drop a few hints or encourage students by rating their guesses "hot" or "cold."

When the answer is guessed or revealed, say, **Why are we talking about dirt? Because dirt, or soil, is the subject of a story Jesus told—a story we are going to take a close look at today. It's called the Parable of the Four Soils, or sometimes the Parable of the Sower. You can find it now in Mark 4:1-20.**

Bible Exploration

EXPLORATION (30-40 minutes)

Materials needed: Your students are going to build four miniature landscapes, as shown in the illustration. The materials you choose depend on their ease of availability, and to a certain extent, your imagination. The more materials you supply, the more fun your students will have (and the bigger mess they will make). Here is a suggested list:

NOTES

Dirt

Pebbles

Modeling clay (for packed earth, rocks, etc.)

Peanuts (to represent the seeds)

Weeds or thorn bush twigs

A wilted flower

Plastic flowers or a healthy flower in a pot

Four boxes (in which to build the landscapes)

Digging tools such as spoons or a trowel

If you have lots of class time, you may wish to supply water and plaster of paris so the students can make permanent displays.

Don't forget paper towels, a trash can and other items necessary for clean up.

You will need something to represent a bird for the hard-packed road landscape. Realistic toy birds can sometimes be found at party supply stores. Or find a picture of a bird, or let the students use colored markers to draw their own. An old shoe would also be fun for the hard-packed road landscape!

Students also need paper and markers to label their creations, as described below.

Step 1 (1 minute): After students have opened their Bibles, read Mark 4:1-20 aloud.

Step 2 (15-20 minutes): Assemble students into four groups. Assign each group a title and passage (written on the chalkboard):

The Crows: Mark 4:4,15
The Rockers; Mark 4:5,6,16,17
The Weeds: Mark 4:7,18,19
The Dirtballs: Mark 4:8,20

These titles are of course intended to be tongue-in-cheek. As you describe the assignment, give each group a box in which to build their landscape. Tell groups to read their assigned verses and brainstorm what sort of landscape they will construct to best illustrate their particular soil. Say, **When you have decided exactly what you wish to make, elect one person to come to me for any materials you need.**

Walk around the classroom as students work, offering advice and encouragement.

OPTIONAL:

If your weather and location permit, take your learners outside and let them hunt up the dirt, rocks, and plants they require. Supervision, of course, is a must.

Step 3 (8-10 minutes): Congratulate students on their efforts. Gather all four boxes in a row for display in the front of the room. Now say something like, **I'm giving each group a sheet of paper and a felt pen. At the top of the page write the title of your box of soil, for example, "The Rocky Soil" or "The Good Soil." Then read your assigned verses again. Rewrite those verses in your own words and print them under the titles.** When students are finished, have one person from each group tape their papers to the boxes.

Step 4 (5-10 minutes): Write on your chalkboard the words shown in the illustration:

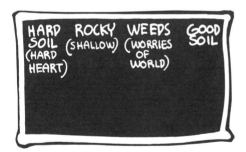

Read the following list of "Modern Soil Samples" to your class. (The purpose of this step is to allow students to relate what they learned in Mark 4:1-20 to the type of people in the world today.) As you read each description, ask students to vote for which soil on the chalkboard best represents the person described. (Some of the persons described can fit more than one category.) As students indicate their preferences, quickly jot them on the chalkboard. Discuss with students their reasons for voting the way they do.

"MODERN SOIL SAMPLES"

The person who says, "I don't need God."

The person who is watching football rather than attending worship service.

The guy who is here to "scheme" on a good-looking girl.

The person who is reading the Bible regularly.

The person who prays.

The junior higher who stops coming because his favorite youth minister moved away.

The person who lives for his car above all else.

The junior higher who hides her Bible when unsaved friends come around.

The junior higher who wants to obey the Lord.

The junior higher who acts like an angel on Sunday—only.

The junior higher who got excited about God because her friends did, and then "bombed out" when they did.

The junior higher who is here because Mom makes him come, but who cares nothing about God.

The junior higher who wants his friends to become Christians.

The junior higher who regularly asks God to forgive her sins.

Conclusion and Decision

CONCLUSION (1 minute)

Tell students to mentally choose one or more people from the "Good Soil" list that they would like God to help them be more like. Close in prayer, asking God to help everyone behave like all the people on the "Good Soil" list so that their lives might be a rich harvest in the service of God.

Distribute the Fun Page take-home paper.

Note: The next session, session 6, requires special preparation and materials. See "BEFORE CLASS BEGINS" on page 78.

=AN IMPORTANT= MESSAGE!

Session 5

What does a person's life amount to if he or she has a cold heart toward God?

To find the answer to this important question, fold the page as shown.

Fold page over like this.

Fold so A meets B.

◀B

A▶

◀B

ZELDA WAVERS TO 'N' FRO BETWEEN SERVING GOD AND IGNORING HIM!

A▶

DAILY NUGGETS Wisdom from God's Word for you to read each day.

Day 1 Read Mark 6:16-28. Why did King Herod have John the Baptist beheaded?

Day 2 Mark 6:45,46. When Jesus sent His disciples ahead of Him in a boat, what did **He** do?

Day 3 Mark 6:48-52. Jesus walked on the lake and the disciples were afraid. Why were they amazed at **Jesus** being able to walk on water?

Day 4 Mark 7:1-8. Whose rules were the Pharisees following and whose should they have been following? Whose do you follow?

Day 5 Mark 7:20-22. What makes a person unclean? Name some of these "unclean" things.

Day 6 Mark 7:24-30. What did the woman ask Jesus to do? How did Jesus respond?

"Others, like seed sown on good soil, hear the word, accept it, and produce a crop—thirty, sixty or even a hundred times what was sown."

Mark 4:20

THEME: Developing a tender heart.

Session 5

BIBLE STUDY OUTLINE

This Popsheet is based on **Ephesians 4:17-5:1, which contrasts the hardness of heart of the unbeliever with the responsiveness to God that the Christian should demonstrate. In this way, the passage goes along with the contrasts Jesus drew in the Parable of the Four Soils studied in the Session Plan which accompanies this Popsheet. Read Ephesians 4:17-5:1 to your students, covering these points as time allows:**

- Ephesians 4:17: Paul, the author of Ephesians, insists "in the Lord" (with the full weight and authority of God), that we no longer live as the average non-Christian does. When God comes into your heart, He makes changes. Some changes happen immediately, some take a lot of effort and time. But our actions and attitudes should definitely become more and more godly.
- Verses 18,19: Paul describes people who do not know God. They are darkened in understanding (unable to see what's really going on); separated from God (a terrible position to be in); hardened (like worthless soil); insensitive (to God and to others); given over to sensuality (the things of this world—which will pass away—instead of the world of eternity); always lusting for more (like a pig that longs for garbage instead of the good food it could have). While a junior higher might not see these things this way, this is the way God sees them. And God is never wrong. People without Christ are in big trouble.
- Verses 21-24: We are commanded to stop being like we used to be before we became Christians, and start being like God. The great thing about this passage is not only is it a command, it's a promise. If God tells us to do something, it must be possible to do. We can live good, clean, godly lives. And this kind of living brings true happiness, instead of the constant search for some phony happiness so many non-Christians go through.
- Verses 25-32: Notice that we are not only commanded to stop doing wrong things, we are told to start doing good (e.g., stop stealing, start working to have something to share; stop speaking bad things, start building up others.). In other words, our CHRISTIANITY should pour out of us into the lives of others. It is not enough to become a Christian and slip into the woodwork. We should be activists—people who are involved and effective. Even people your age can have influence on your friends and families.
- Ephesians 5:1: To imitate means to copy. We should try to live like Jesus did. None of us is perfect, but with Him living through us, we can all become examples of the kind of people Christians are to be.

OBJECT LESSON: THE TREE OF LIFE

Bring a bare branch with lots of little twigs and small branches. Tell students that each time they do something that pleases God, they stay close in toward the trunk, which represents God. But every time they do wrong and choose to go away from God, they branch away from Him. After too many bad choices, they are so far away from the trunk that they might not be able to see it. At that point, even deciding to do right may not immediately set everything right; they are too far away. That is why sin is so dangerous; it leaves Christians out on a dangerous limb.

DISCUSSION QUESTIONS

1. **What are some of the things non-Christians do that Christians shouldn't? Why would these things be wrong? Are they hard for the average Christian to resist?**
2. **In what way could these wrong things lead to unhappiness?**
3. **What sort of things change immediately when a person becomes a Christian? What sort of things take time and effort?**
4. **We have said that we should be activists—involved and concerned. What are some of the things a Christian your age should be involved in and concerned about? What are some practical things you could be doing in school or at home?**

THE COMPLETE JUNIOR HIGH
BIBLE STUDY RESOURCE
BOOK #2

Games taken from the television.

WHEEL OF
MISFORTUNE

Use a chalkboard to play a standard game of "Hangman," with the following modifications.

1. Assemble players into two teams. Teams elect one player each to serve as the representative of the team. Teams may shout instructions to the representatives.

2. The first representative has a chance to spin the "Wheel of Misfortune" (constructed from cardboard as shown). The player gets to guess a letter in the phrase. If the player guesses correctly, he or she gets to "keep" what was earned on the wheel and take another spin. If the player gets a bad item on the wheel, he or she loses the turn. During his or her turn, a player can elect to guess the entire phrase. Team members may help. If the player guesses correctly, the team wins the round. Incorrectly, and the other team gets a chance. If they can't guess, play resumes.

3. Play several rounds, each time adding up how many points the winners have scored on the wheel. At game's end, the team with the most points wins.

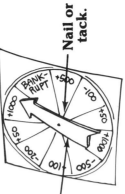

**Nail or
tack.**

Cardboard arrow, about two feet long.

Cardboard or plywood backing (or use bulletin board).

Be sure arrow is perfectly balanced so it won't be "weighted" in any one direction. Tape a quarter to the arrow as a balance weight—use trial and error for correct position.

We recommend you start out with simple, easily recognized phrases until players get the hang of it. Bible verses make good, tough phrases.

25,000 PAZOOTA PYRAMID

The same teams can also play this simple game. One player from each team "gives" (attempts to communicate a concealed word to the other player using one-word definitions or clues); the other player "receives" (attempts to guess the word). Each couple has 30 seconds to communicate five words. Each correctly guessed word counts five points. Words that stump the receiver may be passed to go on to the next word. Call time after exactly 30 seconds and add up the points scored. One couple plays at a time, while the other couple watches. Play several rounds, each time with new couples from the teams. At the end of play, the team with the most points wins.

To give players a bit of a hint, tell them that each of the five words they must guess fall into a certain category (such as words that begin with the letter G, or words from the Bible, and so on.) Prepare index cards with one word on each card. As play progresses, give each "giver" one card at a time. Here is an example of a word to be guessed and the one-word clues a "giver" might use:

Word: **Believe**

Clues: **Trust, faith, accept, convinced, rely.**

Players may use gestures and may reuse any clues.

His Teaching: Self-denial SESSION 6

WHAT THE SESSION IS ABOUT

Selfishness is inconsistent with Christian living.

SCRIPTURE STUDIED

Mark 8:34-38 and many selected verses examined in the course of playing a game.

KEY PASSAGE

"If anyone would come after me, he must deny himself and take up his cross and follow me." Mark 8:34

AIMS OF THE SESSION

During this session your learners will:

1. Examine many verses dealing with self-denial or sharing.
2. Discuss ways junior highers tend to be selfish.
3. Choose one or more areas of selfishness they will work to reduce.

INSIGHTS FOR THE LEADER

Your learners will begin this session by reading what Jesus taught in Mark 8:34: His followers are to deny themselves. Then the entire class will work together for almost the whole class time to play a game (described in the SESSION PLAN) that will cause them to study many passages that speak of self-denial, putting others first, sharing, and the like.

Selfishness

Denying oneself is an adult concept, hard for junior high students to grasp, much less practice. Therefore, this session focuses on the elementary, ground-floor concept that is inherent in self-denial: recognizing and attacking blatant selfishness in oneself. This is something junior highers can understand. They are just coming out of childhood, and they know that children are self-centered. Among the first words a child learns to say are "me" and "mine." A brief observation in a nursery will provide plenty of examples of selfishness.

Junior high students themselves still retain much of the selfishness of childhood. They tend to be greedy and preoccupied with their own interests. They think the world revolves around them. They don't just act that way, they often actually believe it.

At the same time, they are beginning to enter the adult world and to feel the anxieties of growing up, with all the physical and social pressures accompanying the process. These anxieties and pressures sometimes cause them to become more selfish for a time.

Of course, the battle against selfishness is not reserved exclusively for junior highers. All people face it. Perhaps the hardest thing for a Christian to do is to crucify the sinful nature with all its selfish desires. Junior highers have usually learned how to control the outward evidence of selfishness well enough to get along with their peers; but often their inner attitudes haven't changed much since childhood.

Jesus Our Example

Unselfishness involves sacrifice—surrendering our "rights" and desires, and putting the benefit of others ahead of ourselves. Jesus is the ultimate example of self-denial. He is the Christ, the second person of the Godhead, yet He willingly came to earth to live among the human race and to die for our sins. He gave up His rights and His personal convenience in order to benefit us.

Jesus taught His disciples that they, too, must deny themselves. They must take up their crosses and follow Him. Taking up one's cross, in Jesus' day, meant going to one's execution. Jesus' followers must be willing to die for Him. He said, "Whoever wants to save his life will lose it, but whoever loses his life for me and for the gospel will save it. What good is it

for a man to gain the whole world, yet forfeit his soul? Or what can a man give in exchange for his soul?" (vv. 35-37).

Jesus' statement is a paradox. You lose by gaining, or you gain by losing. If you selfishly live your life for yourself, in the end you lose it for eternity. But if you lose your life by giving it to God and allowing Him to control it, you gain eternal life. If you let your selfish desire control your own life, and thus keep you from receiving Christ, you miss out on the glories of eternity. You might gain all the good things this world has to offer, but you lose your soul, the most precious possession a person can have.

Those who are already Christians, yet who allow selfishness to control them, will lose the enjoyment that would be gained from their relationship with the Lord. They won't enjoy talking to Him, reading His Word, or spending time with His people.

Selfishness is too costly. It is far better to begin learning how to overcome selfishness in order to gain something far better—eternal life and the joy of a close walk with God.

SESSION PLAN

BEFORE CLASS BEGINS: You will need three cans or bottles of soft drink and six transparent drinking glasses for the ATTENTION GRABBER. Also, the EXPLORATION and the ALTERNATE EXPLORATION call for special materials. Read the "Stuck!" game instructions on the Teacher's Resource pages. There is no Compass student worksheet for this session.

Attention Grabber

ATTENTION GRABBER (5-6 minutes)

Materials needed: Three cans or bottles of soft drink (chilled, if possible), six transparent drinking glasses.

Ask for three volunteers to come forward to help you with a demonstration. Explain: **I have three cans of soft drink and six glasses. I want the first volunteer to take one soda and two glasses and show me how you would split the drink between yourself and a really cute person of the opposite sex that you want to impress.**

After a bit of lighthearted encouragement, say, **Now I want the second volunteer to come forward and show everyone how you would** split the drink between yourself and a friend.

And now, third volunteer, you will show us how you would split your drink between yourself and someone you don't like.

Tell your students that the object of this little exercise was to point out a truth about human nature: **We are sometimes quite selfish! Even with a soft drink, we don't like to give away more than we have to.** (If your students displayed angelic behavior, you can say, **Many people would pour a little more for themselves if they thought they could get away with it!**) Even up the six glasses of soda and give them to the volunteers and three other students.

Move on to the EXPLORATION by saying something like this: **All of us are selfish. It's part of human nature. We don't want to give a bigger share to someone else, unless there's something in it for us. Followers of Jesus** **need to learn to overcome this selfishness as they grow in Him. That's what we are going to take a look at today as we have some fun playing a game.**

Bible Exploration

EXPLORATION (Variable time)

Materials needed: The "Stuck!" Teacher's Resource pages, cut apart as described on the first page. (You'll need to make photocopies if you have more than 16 students.) A cup, and about 20 tokens (washers or pennies) for each player.

Step 1 (variable time): Play "STUCK!" with your students. See "HOW TO PLAY" printed on the game. Be sure to discuss the meaning and significance of each verse as you read it to your students (the "STUCK!" cards have shortened versions of each verse). Ask students what each verse teaches about selfishness or self-denial.

Play as many games as time allows, with enough time left for Step 2 and the CONCLUSION.

Step 2 (5-6 minutes): Write "How are junior highers selfish?" on the chalkboard and ask students to brainstorm with you ten or more answers. Thank the students for their insights.

ALTERNATE EXPLORATION (20-30 minutes)

Materials needed: Copies of the Fun Page, enough *New International Versions* or *New American Standard Bibles* for each pair of students to have one.

If you prefer not to play "STUCK!", we suggest you allow your students to play the crossword puzzle on the Fun Page. The same passages are covered by both games. As students complete play, discuss the importance and significance of each passage as it relates to selfishness or self-denial. Then do Step 2 of the original EXPLORATION. Conclude this part of the lesson by asking students to prayerfully and individually choose one verse that speaks to their area of greatest need.

Your students may wish to see this solution to the Fun Page puzzle.

(If you like, write the solution on an extra copy of the Fun Page and pin it to your classroom bulletin board.)

Conclusion and Decision

CONCLUSION (2-3 minutes)

Now say, **I want you to each look at your own "STUCK!" card. Choose one or two verses that touch on a problem you've had. For example, if you would like to become a** **more generous person, circle all related verses with your pencil.** Tell your students to keep their cards as a reminder of their commitment.

Close in prayer and distribute the Fun Page.

Note: The next session, session 7, requires some special preparation. See pages 97 and 98 for details.

"STUCK!" A Game of Chance to Help Students Learn the Bible.

PREPARATION: The next page contains a set of 24 cards, each containing a Scripture passage. You the leader will use these cards in the course of playing the game. Cut them out. The following four pages contain 16 "STUCK!" cards, one for each player. (If you have more than 16 students, you will need to copy an extra set or sets and play another game or games elsewhere with other leaders.)

MATERIALS NEEDED: You will need a cup or other container in which to shake the 24 cards, as shown. Students need about 20 player tokens each. Tokens can be pennies or washers. Each player needs one of the "STUCK!" cards. You may wish to offer some reward for the student who wins each game, such as a snack or an inexpensive Christian book.

HOW TO PLAY: When students have arrived, give them each a "STUCK!" card and 20 or so tokens. Tell them that you will draw a Bible verse at random from your cup and read it aloud to them. Each student is to find the matching verse on his or her card and, when they find it, they are to cover it with a token. The object of the game is to be the first player to get five tokens in a row (counting the FREE SPACE in the center of each card). Rows may run vertically, horizontally, or diagonally. The first player to yell, "I'm STUCK!" after getting five in a row is the winner. As you read each verse, allow slow readers enough time to find their verse by discussing the meaning and significance of each. Feel free to ask students questions as you play the game. If time allows more than one game, collect all the "STUCK!" cards after each game, shuffle them, and hand them out again. (Although this serves no purpose as far as the game goes, it may seem more fair to your students.) When the final game has ended, collect all tokens, but allow students to keep the "STUCK!" cards for the CONCLUSION activity.

MARK 8:34 "Then he called the crowd to him along with his disciples and said, 'If anyone would come after me, he must deny himself and take up his cross and follow me.'"	PHILIPPIANS 2:5-7 "Your attitude should be the same as that of Christ Jesus: Who, being in very nature God, did not consider equality with God something to be grasped, but made himself nothing, taking the very nature of a servant, being made in human likeness."	PROVERBS 18:24 "A man of many companions may come to ruin, but there is a friend who sticks closer than a brother."	ROMANS 12:10 "Be devoted to one another in brotherly love. Honor one another above yourselves."
MARK 8:35 "For whoever wants to save his life will lose it, but whoever loses his life for me and for the gospel will save it."	MARK 12:43-44 "Jesus said, 'I tell you the truth, this poor widow has put more into the treasury than all the others. They all gave out of their wealth; but she, out of her poverty, put in everything—all she had to live on.'"	LUKE 14:27 "And anyone who does not carry his cross and follow me cannot be my disciple."	ROMANS 12:13 "Share with God's people who are in need. Practice hospitality."
MARK 8:36 "What good is it for a man to gain the whole world, yet forfeit his soul?"	MATTHEW 4:10 "Jesus said to him, 'Away from me, Satan! For it is written: "Worship the Lord your God, and serve him only."'"	2 CORINTHIANS 5:15 "And he died for all, that those who live should no longer live for themselves but for him who died for them and was raised again."	ROMANS 12:16 "Live in harmony with one another. Do not be proud, but be willing to associate with people of low position."
ROMANS 15:1,2 "We who are strong ought to bear with the failings of the weak and not to please ourselves. Each of us should please his neighbor for his good, to build him up."	PHILIPPIANS 3:7 "But whatever was to my profit I now consider loss for the sake of Christ."	1 PETER 2:13 "Submit yourselves for the Lord's sake to every authority instituted among men."	GALATIANS 5:14 "The entire law is summed up in a single command: 'Love your neighbor as yourself.'"
ROMANS 6:6,7 "For we know that our old self was crucified with him so that the body of sin might be done away with, that we should no longer be slaves to sin—because anyone who has died has been freed from sin."	PSALM 37:21 "The wicked borrow and do not repay, but the righteous give generously."	1 CORINTHIANS 13:4 "Love is patient, love is kind. It does not envy, it does not boast, it is not proud."	GALATIANS 6:2 "Carry each other's burdens, and in this way you will fulfill the law of Christ."
PHILIPPIANS 2:4 "Each of you should look not only to your own interests, but also to the interests of others."	ACTS 2:44,45 "All the believers were together and had everything in common. Selling their possessions and goods, they gave to anyone as he had need."	1 CORINTHIANS 13:5 "[Love] is not rude, it is not self-seeking, it is not easily angered, it keeps no record of wrongs."	GALATIANS 6:9,10 "Let us not become weary in doing good, for at the proper time we will reap a harvest if we do not give up. Therefore, as we have opportunity, let us do good to all people, especially to those who belong to the family of believers."

Are you STUCK? Stuck on yourself, that is? Self-centered, selfish. Well, not too much, we hope—but there's always a lot of room for improvement! As your teacher reads the verses, find them on this card and put your tokens on them. If you get five in a row, you win. These verses are wisdom for selfish people, people who are

STUCK!

1 PETER 2:13 "Submit yourselves for the Lord's sake to every authority."	ROMANS 12:16 "Be willing to associate with people of low position."	ROMANS 12:13 "Share with God's people who are in need."	PSALM 37:21 "The righteous give generously."	MARK 8:34 "If anyone would come after me, he must deny himself."
MARK 12:41-44 "This poor widow has put more into the treasury than all the others."	1 CORINTHIANS 13:5 "[Love] is not self-seeking."	ACTS 2:44,45 "They gave to anyone as he had need."	PHILIPPIANS 2:4 "Each of you should look . . . to the interests of others."	GALATIANS 6:2 "Carry each other's burdens."
MATTHEW 4:10 "Worship the Lord your God, and serve Him only."	GALATIANS 6:9,10 "Let us do good to all people."	FREE SPACE	GALATIANS 5:14 "Love your neighbor as yourself."	PHILIPPIANS 2:5 "Your attitude should be the same as that of Christ Jesus."
ROMANS 12:10 "Be devoted to one another in brotherly love."	LUKE 14:27 "And anyone who does not carry his cross and follow me cannot be my disciple."	1 CORINTHIANS 13:4 "Love is kind."	ROMANS 15:2 "Each of us should please his neighbor."	MARK 8:36 "What good is it for a man to gain the whole world, yet forfeit his soul?"
PROVERBS 18:24 "There is a friend who sticks closer than a brother."	ROMANS 6:6 "We know that our old self was crucified with him."	MARK 8:35 "Whoever loses his life for me and for the gospel will save it."	2 CORINTHIANS 5:15 "Those who live should no longer live for themselves."	PHILIPPIANS 3:7 "But whatever was to my profit I now consider loss."

Are you STUCK? Stuck on yourself, that is? Self-centered, selfish. Well, not too much, we hope—but there's always a lot of room for improvement! As your teacher reads the verses, find them on this card and put your tokens on them. If you get five in a row, you win. These verses are wisdom for selfish people, people who are

STUCK!

ROMANS 12:10 "Be devoted to one another in brotherly love."	MATTHEW 4:10 "Worship the Lord your God, and serve Him only."	PHILIPPIANS 3:7 "But whatever was to my profit I now consider loss."	PROVERBS 18:24 "There is a friend who sticks closer than a brother."	ACTS 2:44,45 "They gave to anyone as he had need."
1 PETER 2:13 "Submit yourselves for the Lord's sake to every authority."	1 CORINTHIANS 13:5 "[Love] is not self-seeking."	1 CORINTHIANS 13:4 "Love is kind."	PHILIPPIANS 2:4 "Each of you should look . . . to the interests of others."	MARK 8:35 "Whoever loses his life for me and for the gospel will save it."
MARK 12:41-44 "This poor widow has put more into the treasury than all the others."	GALATIANS 6:9,10 "Let us do good to all people."	FREE SPACE	ROMANS 12:13 "Share with God's people who are in need."	PHILIPPIANS 2:5 "Your attitude should be the same as that of Christ Jesus."
ROMANS 6:6 "We know that our old self was crucified with him."	LUKE 14:27 "And anyone who does not carry his cross and follow me cannot be my disciple."	GALATIANS 6:2 "Carry each other's burdens."	ROMANS 15:2 "Each of us should please his neighbor."	MARK 8:36 "What good is it for a man to gain the whole world, yet forfeit his soul?"
MARK 8:34 "If anyone would come after me, he must deny himself."	ROMANS 12:16 "Be willing to associate with people of low position."	PSALM 37:21 "The righteous give generously."	2 CORINTHIANS 5:15 "Those who live should no longer live for themselves."	GALATIANS 5:14 "Love your neighbor as yourself."

Are you STUCK? Stuck on yourself, that is? Self-centered, selfish. Well, not too much, we hope—but there's always a lot of room for improvement! As your teacher reads the verses, find them on this card and put your tokens on them. If you get five in a row, you win. These verses are wisdom for selfish people, people who are

STUCK!

1 PETER 2:13 "Submit yourselves for the Lord's sake to every authority."	ROMANS 15:2 "Each of us should please his neighbor."	ROMANS 12:10 "Be devoted to one another in brotherly love."	ROMANS 6:6 "We know that our old self was crucified with him."	MARK 8:34 "If anyone would come after me, he must deny himself."
ACTS 2:44,45 "They gave to anyone as he had need."	PSALM 37:21 "The righteous give generously."	ROMANS 12:13 "Share with God's people who are in need."	MATTHEW 4:10 "Worship the Lord your God, and serve Him only."	MARK 8:35 "Whoever loses his life for me and for the gospel will save it."
GALATIANS 5:14 "Love your neighbor as yourself."	1 CORINTHIANS 13:4 "Love is kind."	FREE SPACE	GALATIANS 6:9,10 "Let us do good to all people."	PHILIPPIANS 2:5 "Your attitude should be the same as that of Christ Jesus."
1 CORINTHIANS 13:5 "[Love] is not self-seeking."	LUKE 14:27 "And anyone who does not carry his cross and follow me cannot be my disciple."	GALATIANS 6:2 "Carry each other's burdens."	ROMANS 12:16 "Be willing to associate with people of low position."	MARK 8:36 "What good is it for a man to gain the whole world, yet forfeit his soul?"
PROVERBS 18:24 "There is a friend who sticks closer than a brother."	PHILIPPIANS 2:4 "Each of you should look . . . to the interests of others."	MARK 12:41-44 "This poor widow has put more into the treasury than all the others."	2 CORINTHIANS 5:15 "Those who live should no longer live for themselves."	PHILIPPIANS 3:7 "But whatever was to my profit I now consider loss."

Are you STUCK? Stuck on yourself, that is? Self-centered, selfish. Well, not too much, we hope—but there's always a lot of room for improvement! As your teacher reads the verses, find them on this card and put your tokens on them. If you get five in a row, you win. These verses are wisdom for selfish people, people who are

STUCK!

1 CORINTHIANS 13:4 "Love is kind."	ROMANS 12:16 "Be willing to associate with people of low position."	GALATIANS 5:14 "Love your neighbor as yourself."	PSALM 37:21 "The righteous give generously."	GALATIANS 6:2 "Carry each other's burdens."
ACTS 2:44,45 "They gave to anyone as he had need."	1 CORINTHIANS 13:5 "[Love] is not self-seeking."	PROVERBS 18:24 "There is a friend who sticks closer than a brother."	PHILIPPIANS 2:4 "Each of you should look . . . to the interests of others."	MARK 8:35 "Whoever loses his life for me and for the gospel will save it."
MATTHEW 4:10 "Worship the Lord your God, and serve Him only."	PHILIPPIANS 3:7 "But whatever was to my profit I now consider loss."	FREE SPACE	1 PETER 2:13 "Submit yourselves for the Lord's sake to every authority."	PHILIPPIANS 2:5 "Your attitude should be the same as that of Christ Jesus."
ROMANS 12:10 "Be devoted to one another in brotherly love."	LUKE 14:27 "And anyone who does not carry his cross and follow me cannot be my disciple."	MARK 8:34 "If anyone would come after me, he must deny himself."	ROMANS 15:2 "Each of us should please his neighbor."	MARK 8:36 "What good is it for a man to gain the whole world, yet forfeit his soul?"
ROMANS 12:13 "Share with God's people who are in need."	ROMANS 6:6 "We know that our old self was crucified with him."	MARK 12:41-44 "This poor widow has put more into the treasury than all the others."	2 CORINTHIANS 5:15 "Those who live should no longer live for themselves."	GALATIANS 6:9,10 "Let us do good to all people."

Card 1 (top-left)

Are you STUCK? Stuck on yourself, that is? Self-centered, selfish. Well, not too much, we hope—but there's always a lot of room for improvement! As your teacher reads the verses, find them on this card and put your tokens on them. If you get five in a row, you win. These verses are wisdom for selfish people, people who are

STUCK!

1 PETER 2:13 "Submit yourselves for the Lord's sake to every authority."	ROMANS 12:16 "Be willing to associate with people of low position."	MARK 8:35 "Whoever loses his life for me and for the gospel will save it."	PHILIPPIANS 2:5 "Your attitude should be the same as that of Christ Jesus."	MARK 8:34 "If anyone would come after me, he must deny himself."
GALATIANS 6:2 "Carry each other's burdens."	1 CORINTHIANS 13:5 "[Love] is not self-seeking."	PHILIPPIANS 2:4 "Each of you should look . . . to the interests of others."	1 CORINTHIANS 13:4 "Love is kind."	PROVERBS 18:24 "There is a friend who sticks closer than a brother."
MATTHEW 4:10 "Worship the Lord your God, and serve Him only."	ROMANS 6:6 "We know that our old self was crucified with him."	FREE SPACE	ROMANS 15:2 "Each of us should please his neighbor."	GALATIANS 5:14 "Love your neighbor as yourself."
ROMANS 12:10 "Be devoted to one another in brotherly love."	LUKE 14:27 "And anyone who does not carry his cross and follow me cannot be my disciple."	GALATIANS 6:9,10 "Let us do good to all people."	ROMANS 12:13 "Share with God's people who are in need."	MARK 8:36 "What good is it for a man to gain the whole world, yet forfeit his soul?"
PSALM 37:21 "The righteous give generously."	ACTS 2:44,45 "They gave to anyone as he had need."	MARK 12:41-44 "This poor widow has put more into the treasury than all the others."	2 CORINTHIANS 5:15 "Those who live should live no longer live for themselves."	PHILIPPIANS 3:7 "But whatever was to my profit I now consider loss."

Card 2 (top-right)

Are you STUCK? Stuck on yourself, that is? Self-centered, selfish. Well, not too much, we hope—but there's always a lot of room for improvement! As your teacher reads the verses, find them on this card and put your tokens on them. If you get five in a row, you win. These verses are wisdom for selfish people, people who are

STUCK!

MATTHEW 4:10 "Worship the Lord your God, and serve Him only."	ROMANS 12:13 "Share with God's people who are in need."	GALATIANS 6:2 "Carry each other's burdens."	1 PETER 2:13 "Submit yourselves for the Lord's sake to every authority."	MARK 8:34 "If anyone would come after me, he must deny himself."
PHILIPPIANS 2:4 "Each of you should look . . . to the interests of others."	1 CORINTHIANS 13:4 "Love is kind."	1 CORINTHIANS 13:5 "[Love] is not self-seeking."	PSALM 37:21 "The righteous give generously."	2 CORINTHIANS 5:15 "Those who live should live no longer live for themselves."
ROMANS 12:16 "Be willing to associate with people of low position."	FREE SPACE	GALATIANS 6:9,10 "Let us do good to all people."	MARK 8:35 "Whoever loses his life for me and for the gospel will save it."	PHILIPPIANS 2:5 "Your attitude should be the same as that of Christ Jesus."
ROMANS 15:2 "Each of us should please his neighbor."	ACTS 2:44,45 "They gave to anyone as he had need."	LUKE 14:27 "And anyone who does not carry his cross and follow me cannot be my disciple."	GALATIANS 5:14 "Love your neighbor as yourself."	MARK 8:36 "What good is it for a man to gain the whole world, yet forfeit his soul?"
PHILIPPIANS 3:7 "But whatever was to my profit I now consider loss."	MARK 12:41-44 "This poor widow has put more into the treasury than all the others."	ROMANS 6:6 "We know that our old self was crucified with him."	PROVERBS 18:24 "There is a friend who sticks closer than a brother."	ROMANS 12:10 "Be devoted to one another in brotherly love."

Card 3 (bottom-left)

Are you STUCK? Stuck on yourself, that is? Self-centered, selfish. Well, not too much, we hope—but there's always a lot of room for improvement! As your teacher reads the verses, find them on this card and put your tokens on them. If you get five in a row, you win. These verses are wisdom for selfish people, people who are

STUCK!

1 PETER 2:13 "Submit yourselves for the Lord's sake to every authority."	ROMANS 12:16 "Be willing to associate with people of low position."	MARK 8:35 "Whoever loses his life for me and for the gospel will save it."	PHILIPPIANS 2:5 "Your attitude should be the same as that of Christ Jesus."	MARK 8:34 "If anyone would come after me, he must deny himself."
GALATIANS 6:2 "Carry each other's burdens."	1 CORINTHIANS 13:5 "[Love] is not self-seeking."	ROMANS 6:6 "We know that our old self was crucified with him."	1 CORINTHIANS 13:4 "Love is kind."	PROVERBS 18:24 "There is a friend who sticks closer than a brother."
MATTHEW 4:10 "Worship the Lord your God, and serve Him only."	FREE SPACE	GALATIANS 6:9,10 "Let us do good to all people."	ROMANS 15:2 "Each of us should please his neighbor."	GALATIANS 5:14 "Love your neighbor as yourself."
ROMANS 12:10 "Be devoted to one another in brotherly love."	LUKE 14:27 "And anyone who does not carry his cross and follow me cannot be my disciple."	ROMANS 12:13 "Share with God's people who are in need."	MARK 12:41-44 "This poor widow has put more into the treasury than all the others."	MARK 8:36 "What good is it for a man to gain the whole world, yet forfeit his soul?"
PSALM 37:21 "The righteous give generously."	ACTS 2:44,45 "They gave to anyone as he had need."	PHILIPPIANS 2:4 "Each of you should look . . . to the interests of others."	2 CORINTHIANS 5:15 "Those who live should live no longer live for themselves."	PHILIPPIANS 3:7 "But whatever was to my profit I now consider loss."

Card 4 (bottom-right)

Are you STUCK? Stuck on yourself, that is? Self-centered, selfish. Well, not too much, we hope—but there's always a lot of room for improvement! As your teacher reads the verses, find them on this card and put your tokens on them. If you get five in a row, you win. These verses are wisdom for selfish people, people who are

STUCK!

ROMANS 12:16 "Be willing to associate with people of low position."	PHILIPPIANS 3:7 "But whatever was to my profit I now consider loss."	MARK 12:41-44 "This poor widow has put more into the treasury than all the others."	PROVERBS 18:24 "There is a friend who sticks closer than a brother."	LUKE 14:27 "And anyone who does not carry his cross and follow me cannot be my disciple."
GALATIANS 6:2 "Carry each other's burdens."	PHILIPPIANS 2:4 "Each of you should look . . . to the interests of others."	ROMANS 15:2 "Each of us should please his neighbor."	MARK 8:34 "If anyone would come after me, he must deny himself."	ROMANS 12:10 "Be devoted to one another in brotherly love."
MATTHEW 4:10 "Worship the Lord your God, and serve Him only."	MARK 8:35 "Whoever loses his life for me and for the gospel will save it."	FREE SPACE	ROMANS 12:13 "Share with God's people who are in need."	GALATIANS 5:14 "Love your neighbor as yourself."
PSALM 37:21 "The righteous give generously."	PHILIPPIANS 2:5 "Your attitude should be the same as that of Christ Jesus."	1 CORINTHIANS 13:4 "Love is kind."	MARK 8:36 "What good is it for a man to gain the whole world, yet forfeit his soul?"	ACTS 2:44,45 "They gave to anyone as he had need."
1 PETER 2:13 "Submit yourselves for the Lord's sake to every authority."	1 CORINTHIANS 13:5 "[Love] is not self-seeking."	GALATIANS 6:9,10 "Let us do good to all people."	2 CORINTHIANS 5:15 "Those who live should live no longer live for themselves."	ROMANS 6:6 "We know that our old self was crucified with him."

Each of the four cards below carries the same introductory text:

> Are you STUCK? Stuck on yourself, that is? Self-centered, selfish. Well, not too much, we hope—but there's always a lot of room for improvement! As your teacher reads the verses, find them on this card and put your tokens on them. If you get five in a row, you win. These verses are wisdom for selfish people, people who are

STUCK!

Card 1

GALATIANS 6:9,10 "Let us do good to all people."	2 CORINTHIANS 5:15 "Those who live should no longer live for themselves."	GALATIANS 6:2 "Carry each other's burdens."	PSALM 37:21 "The righteous give generously."	MARK 8:34 "If anyone would come after me, he must deny himself."
LUKE 14:27 "And anyone who does not carry his cross and follow me cannot be my disciple."	ACTS 2:44,45 "They gave to anyone as he had need."	PHILIPPIANS 3:7 "But whatever was to my profit I now consider loss."	PHILIPPIANS 2:4 "Each of you should look . . . to the interests of others."	MARK 8:35 "Whoever loses his life for me and for the gospel will save it."
1 CORINTHIANS 13:4 "Love is kind."	MATTHEW 4:10 "Worship the Lord your God, and serve Him only."	FREE SPACE	ROMANS 12:13 "Share with God's people who are in need."	PHILIPPIANS 2:5 "Your attitude should be the same as that of Christ Jesus."
ROMANS 15:2 "Each of us should please his neighbor."	ROMANS 6:6 "We know that our old self was crucified with him."	ROMANS 12:16 "Be willing to associate with people of low position."	ROMANS 12:10 "Be devoted to one another in brotherly love."	MARK 8:36 "What good is it for a man to gain the whole world, yet forfeit his soul?"
MARK 12:41-44 "This poor widow has put more into the treasury than all the others."	PROVERBS 18:24 "There is a friend who sticks closer than a brother."	1 CORINTHIANS 13:5 "[Love] is not self-seeking."	1 PETER 2:13 "Submit yourselves for the Lord's sake to every authority."	GALATIANS 5:14 "Love your neighbor as yourself."

Card 2

1 PETER 2:13 "Submit yourselves for the Lord's sake to every authority."	ROMANS 12:16 "Be willing to associate with people of low position."	GALATIANS 5:14 "Love your neighbor as yourself."	PSALM 37:21 "The righteous give generously."	MARK 8:34 "If anyone would come after me, he must deny himself."
ACTS 2:44,45 "They gave to anyone as he had need."	1 CORINTHIANS 13:5 "[Love] is not self-seeking."	1 CORINTHIANS 13:4 "Love is kind."	PHILIPPIANS 2:4 "Each of you should look . . . to the interests of others."	MARK 8:35 "Whoever loses his life for me and for the gospel will save it."
MATTHEW 4:10 "Worship the Lord your God, and serve Him only."	GALATIANS 6:9,10 "Let us do good to all people."	FREE SPACE	ROMANS 12:13 "Share with God's people who are in need."	PHILIPPIANS 2:5 "Your attitude should be the same as that of Christ Jesus."
ROMANS 12:10 "Be devoted to one another in brotherly love."	LUKE 14:27 "And anyone who does not carry his cross and follow me cannot be my disciple."	GALATIANS 6:2 "Carry each other's burdens."	ROMANS 15:2 "Each of us should please his neighbor."	MARK 8:36 "What good is it for a man to gain the whole world, yet forfeit his soul?"
PROVERBS 18:24 "There is a friend who sticks closer than a brother."	ROMANS 6:6 "We know that our old self was crucified with him."	MARK 12:41-44 "This poor widow has put more into the treasury than all the others."	2 CORINTHIANS 5:15 "Those who live should no longer live for themselves."	PHILIPPIANS 3:7 "But whatever was to my profit I now consider loss."

Card 3

1 CORINTHIANS 13:5 "[Love] is not self-seeking."	ROMANS 12:16 "Be willing to associate with people of low position."	GALATIANS 5:14 "Love your neighbor as yourself."	PSALM 37:21 "The righteous give generously."	MARK 8:34 "If anyone would come after me, he must deny himself."
ACTS 2:44,45 "They gave to anyone as he had need."	PROVERBS 18:24 "There is a friend who sticks closer than a brother."	1 CORINTHIANS 13:4 "Love is kind."	PHILIPPIANS 2:4 "Each of you should look . . . to the interests of others."	MARK 8:35 "Whoever loses his life for me and for the gospel will save it."
MATTHEW 4:10 "Worship the Lord your God, and serve Him only."	GALATIANS 6:9,10 "Let us do good to all people."	FREE SPACE	ROMANS 12:13 "Share with God's people who are in need."	PHILIPPIANS 2:5 "Your attitude should be the same as that of Christ Jesus."
ROMANS 12:10 "Be devoted to one another in brotherly love."	ROMANS 15:2 "Each of us should please his neighbor."	GALATIANS 6:2 "Carry each other's burdens."	ROMANS 6:6 "We know that our old self was crucified with him."	MARK 8:36 "What good is it for a man to gain the whole world, yet forfeit his soul?"
LUKE 14:27 "And anyone who does not carry his cross and follow me cannot be my disciple."	1 PETER 2:13 "Submit yourselves for the Lord's sake to every authority."	MARK 12:41-44 "This poor widow has put more into the treasury than all the others."	2 CORINTHIANS 5:15 "Those who live should no longer live for themselves."	PHILIPPIANS 3:7 "But whatever was to my profit I now consider loss."

Card 4

PHILIPPIANS 3:7 "But whatever was to my profit I now consider loss."	ROMANS 12:13 "Share with God's people who are in need."	GALATIANS 5:14 "Love your neighbor as yourself."	GALATIANS 6:2 "Carry each other's burdens."	PROVERBS 18:24 "There is a friend who sticks closer than a brother."
ACTS 2:44,45 "They gave to anyone as he had need."	1 CORINTHIANS 13:5 "[Love] is not self-seeking."	2 CORINTHIANS 5:15 "Those who live should no longer live for themselves."	PHILIPPIANS 2:4 "Each of you should look . . . to the interests of others."	MARK 8:35 "Whoever loses his life for me and for the gospel will save it."
1 CORINTHIANS 13:4 "Love is kind."	MARK 12:41-44 "This poor widow has put more into the treasury than all the others."	FREE SPACE	PSALM 37:21 "The righteous give generously."	MARK 8:34 "If anyone would come after me, he must deny himself."
ROMANS 12:10 "Be devoted to one another in brotherly love."	ROMANS 12:16 "Be willing to associate with people of low position."	LUKE 14:27 "And anyone who does not carry his cross and follow me cannot be my disciple."	ROMANS 15:2 "Each of us should please his neighbor."	MARK 8:36 "What good is it for a man to gain the whole world, yet forfeit his soul?"
GALATIANS 6:9,10 "Let us do good to all people."	1 PETER 2:13 "Submit yourselves for the Lord's sake to every authority."	MATTHEW 4:10 "Worship the Lord your God, and serve Him only."	PHILIPPIANS 2:5 "Your attitude should be the same as that of Christ Jesus."	ROMANS 6:6 "We know that our old self was crucified with him."

Are you STUCK? Stuck on yourself, that is? Self-centered, selfish. Well, not too much, we hope—but there's always a lot of room for improvement! As your teacher reads the verses, find them on this card and put your tokens on them. If you get five in a row, you win. These verses are wisdom for selfish people, people who are

STUCK!

1 CORINTHIANS 13:5 "[Love] is not self-seeking."	ROMANS 12:16 "Be willing to associate with people of low position."	PHILIPPIANS 2:5 "Your attitude should be the same as that of Christ Jesus."	PSALM 37:21 "The righteous give generously."	MATTHEW 4:10 "Worship the Lord your God, and serve Him only."
ACTS 2:44,45 "They gave to anyone as he had need."	GALATIANS 6:2 "Carry each other's burdens."	1 CORINTHIANS 13:4 "Love is kind."	MARK 8:34 "If anyone would come after me, he must deny himself."	MARK 8:35 "Whoever loses his life for me and for the gospel will save it."
ROMANS 15:2 "Each of us should please his neighbor."	GALATIANS 6:9,10 "Let us do good to all people."	FREE SPACE	ROMANS 12:13 "Share with God's people who are in need."	ROMANS 12:13 "Be devoted to one another in brotherly love."
GALATIANS 5:14 "Love your neighbor as yourself."	LUKE 14:27 "And anyone who does not carry his cross and follow me cannot be my disciple."	PHILIPPIANS 3:7 "But whatever was to my profit I now consider loss."	ROMANS 6:6 "We know that our old self was crucified with him."	MARK 8:36 "What good is it for a man to gain the whole world, yet forfeit his soul?"
PROVERBS 18:24 "There is a friend who sticks closer than a brother."	PHILIPPIANS 2:4 "Each of you should look... to the interests of others."	MARK 12:41-44 "This poor widow has put more into the treasury than all the others."	2 CORINTHIANS 5:15 "Those who live should live no longer for themselves."	1 PETER 2:13 "Submit yourselves for the Lord's sake to every authority."

Are you STUCK? Stuck on yourself, that is? Self-centered, selfish. Well, not too much, we hope—but there's always a lot of room for improvement! As your teacher reads the verses, find them on this card and put your tokens on them. If you get five in a row, you win. These verses are wisdom for selfish people, people who are

STUCK!

1 PETER 2:13 "Submit yourselves for the Lord's sake to every authority."	GALATIANS 5:14 "Love your neighbor as yourself."	MARK 8:34 "If anyone would come after me, he must deny himself."	ACTS 2:44,45 "They gave to anyone as he had need."	MATTHEW 4:10 "Worship the Lord your God, and serve Him only."
ROMANS 12:16 "Be willing to associate with people of low position."	ROMANS 12:10 "Be devoted to one another in brotherly love."	MARK 12:41-44 "This poor widow has put more into the treasury than all the others."	PHILIPPIANS 2:4 "Each of you should look... to the interests of others."	MARK 8:35 "Whoever loses his life for me and for the gospel will save it."
MATTHEW 4:10 "Worship the Lord your God, and serve Him only."	PSALM 37:21 "The righteous give generously."	FREE SPACE	PHILIPPIANS 2:5 "Your attitude should be the same as that of Christ Jesus."	ROMANS 12:13 "Share with God's people who are in need."
ROMANS 12:16 "Be willing to associate with people of low position."	LUKE 14:27 "And anyone who does not carry his cross and follow me cannot be my disciple."	MARK 8:35 "Whoever loses his life for me and for the gospel will save it."	MARK 8:36 "What good is it for a man to gain the whole world, yet forfeit his soul?"	ROMANS 15:2 "Each of us should please his neighbor."
PROVERBS 18:24 "There is a friend who sticks closer than a brother."	1 CORINTHIANS 13:4 "Love is kind."	GALATIANS 6:2 "Carry each other's burdens."	1 CORINTHIANS 13:5 "[Love] is not self-seeking."	2 CORINTHIANS 5:15 "Those who live should live no longer for themselves."

Are you STUCK? Stuck on yourself, that is? Self-centered, selfish. Well, not too much, we hope—but there's always a lot of room for improvement! As your teacher reads the verses, find them on this card and put your tokens on them. If you get five in a row, you win. These verses are wisdom for selfish people, people who are

STUCK!

1 PETER 2:13 "Submit yourselves for the Lord's sake to every authority."	GALATIANS 6:9,10 "Let us do good to all people."	GALATIANS 5:14 "Love your neighbor as yourself."	ACTS 2:44,45 "They gave to anyone as he had need."	MARK 8:34 "If anyone would come after me, he must deny himself."
ROMANS 6:6 "We know that our old self was crucified with him."	1 CORINTHIANS 13:5 "[Love] is not self-seeking."	ROMANS 12:10 "Be devoted to one another in brotherly love."	PHILIPPIANS 2:4 "Each of you should look... to the interests of others."	MARK 12:41-44 "This poor widow has put more into the treasury than all the others."
1 CORINTHIANS 13:4 "Love is kind."	PSALM 37:21 "The righteous give generously."	FREE SPACE	ROMANS 12:13 "Share with God's people who are in need."	PHILIPPIANS 2:5 "Your attitude should be the same as that of Christ Jesus."
ROMANS 12:10 "Be devoted to one another in brotherly love."	LUKE 14:27 "And anyone who does not carry his cross and follow me cannot be my disciple."	MARK 8:35 "Whoever loses his life for me and for the gospel will save it."	ROMANS 15:2 "Each of us should please his neighbor."	MARK 8:36 "What good is it for a man to gain the whole world, yet forfeit his soul?"
ROMANS 12:16 "Be willing to associate with people of low position."	1 CORINTHIANS 13:4 "Love is kind."	GALATIANS 6:2 "Carry each other's burdens."	1 CORINTHIANS 13:4 "Love is kind."	PROVERBS 18:24 "There is a friend who sticks closer than a brother."

Are you STUCK? Stuck on yourself, that is? Self-centered, selfish. Well, not too much, we hope—but there's always a lot of room for improvement! As your teacher reads the verses, find them on this card and put your tokens on them. If you get five in a row, you win. These verses are wisdom for selfish people, people who are

STUCK!

1 PETER 2:13 "Submit yourselves for the Lord's sake to every authority."	ACTS 2:44,45 "They gave to anyone as he had need."	MATTHEW 4:10 "Worship the Lord your God, and serve Him only."	GALATIANS 5:14 "Love your neighbor as yourself."	MARK 8:34 "If anyone would come after me, he must deny himself."
ROMANS 12:16 "Be willing to associate with people of low position."	ROMANS 6:6 "We know that our old self was crucified with him."	ROMANS 15:2 "Each of us should please his neighbor."	ROMANS 12:10 "Be devoted to one another in brotherly love."	MARK 8:35 "Whoever loses his life for me and for the gospel will save it."
1 CORINTHIANS 13:5 "[Love] is not self-seeking."	PSALM 37:21 "The righteous give generously."	FREE SPACE	1 CORINTHIANS 13:4 "Love is kind."	GALATIANS 6:2 "Carry each other's burdens."
ROMANS 12:10 "Be devoted to one another in brotherly love."	PHILIPPIANS 2:4 "Each of you should look... to the interests of others."	LUKE 14:27 "And anyone who does not carry his cross and follow me cannot be my disciple."	PHILIPPIANS 2:5 "Your attitude should be the same as that of Christ Jesus."	MARK 8:36 "What good is it for a man to gain the whole world, yet forfeit his soul?"
ROMANS 12:13 "Share with God's people who are in need."	PROVERBS 18:24 "There is a friend who sticks closer than a brother."	MARK 12:41-44 "This poor widow has put more into the treasury than all the others."	MARK 8:35 "Whoever loses his life for me and for the gospel will save it."	GALATIANS 6:9,10 "Let us do good to all people."

DENY IT!

Jesus said we have to deny ourselves if we really want to be one of His disciples (that's in Mark 8:34). A big part of self-denial is . . . well, if you work this crossword, you'll see many things that are a part of self-denial. You'll need a Bible to solve the clues. We recommend the *New American Standard* or *New International Version*; other versions may have slightly different words (but will probably work anyway).

ACROSS

3. Acts 2:44,45. All the believers were sharing everything in _____.
5. Mark 12:41-44. The _____ put in all she had.
8. Galatians 6:2. We should carry these for each other.
10. 2 Corinthians 5:15. Jesus died so that people would no longer live for _____.
13. People should be able to depend _____ us.
14. When asked to do a favor, say _____.
15. Romans 12:13. We are to practice _____.
18. Galatians 5:14. "_____ your neighbor as yourself."
20. Philippians 3:7. Paul considers everything _____ for the sake of Christ.
22. Romans 12:10. We are to be _____ to each other.
23. Luke 14:27. If you carry your cross, you can be His _____.
24. Matthew 4:10. You should worship and _____ God only. (One way to do this is by helping others.)

DOWN

1. Galatians 5:14. "Love your neighbor as _____."
2. 1 Peter 2:13. We are supposed to _____ to the government.
4. Mark 12:41-44. This is a good thing to be generous with.
6. Philippians 2:4 We should look out for the _____ of others.
7. Romans 12:16. We must be willing to _____ with people of low position.
8. Romans 15:2. We should _____ each other up.
9. Mark 8:34. We must _____ ourselves.
11. 2 Corinthians 5:15. Jesus died so that people would no longer _____ for themselves.
12. Another world for "hey."
13. Philippians 2:4. Whose good should we seek?
16. Romans 15:1,2. We should do what to our neighbor for his own good?
17. Galatians 6:9,10. We should do this to all people.
19. Romans 15:1. We ought to _____ with others failings.
21. Mark 8:35. What happens if you lose your life for Christ?

DAILY NUGGETS

Day 1 Read Mark 8:14-21. Like the disciples, do you sometimes have trouble knowing what God is telling you?

Day 2 Mark 8:22-26. List a couple of things you see more clearly (understand better) now than before you became a Christian?

Day 3 Mark 8:27,28. Who did the people say Jesus was? Who do you think He is?

Day 4 Mark 8:31-33. Why do you suppose Jesus spoke to Peter the way He did?

Day 5 Mark 8:34-38. What must you do to follow Jesus?

Day 6 Mark 9:1-12. What did the voice from the cloud say? How would a person listen to Jesus today?

"If anyone would come after me, he must deny himself and take up his cross and follow me."

Mark 8:34

THEME: Selflessness requires sacrifice.

Session 6

BIBLE STUDY OUTLINE

Read the story of the widow's offering, Mark 12:41-44. Make these points as time allows:

- Verse 41: Jesus was sitting in the Temple. He often taught there, and at that time He was very popular with the crowds. He was popular because He taught with power. His words had the ability to change hearts and lives. That power still exists in His words that we read even now. If you listen carefully to Him, your life will also be changed.
- Many rich people threw in large amounts of money. What were the motives in their hearts? Some undoubtedly did it to try to win favor with God. Perhaps others wanted to impress their friends or onlookers. Some may truly have cared about contributing to God's Temple. But each and every one of them gave out of their surplus; they could easily afford what they gave, it was no skin off their nose (see v. 44).
- Verses 42-44: Notice that Jesus compared these two almost worthless coins to all that wealth: The widow had put in more. Not more in the eyes of bankers and financiers, but more in the sight of God, which is what counts. She didn't put in her surplus—she put in all that she had. She gave **sacrificially**. It wasn't much, but it was everything. And that's what God expects us to do with our lives. We might not be big, important people right now, but when we give our lives to God, He treats us as if we are the most important people in the universe.
- Galatians 6:7-10: We reap what we sow—if we give, God will give to us. Verse 9 tells us that God has a "proper time" when He will settle accounts with us. Because of this, we are to do good to all people, especially believers. God will pay us back according to our generosity or lack of it. Sometimes we don't like to wait to be repaid, but God will repay—and we can't out-give our generous Lord.

TRUE STORY: MIKE AND THE TEDDY BEAR

Mike lived in a home for the severely handicapped; he was physically unable to care for himself. His bent body had to be tied into the wheelchair with towels. Someone had to feed him; someone had to take him to the bathroom. He couldn't speak, except high-pitched squeals. In the eyes of the world, he was a man to be pitied and avoided. He was defective, deficient—a "loser." At least, that's what most people would say.

He was also very poor. Everything he had came from the government. They paid his medical bills, and for his food and a few clothes. They gave him nothing else. The only possession he had that he really treasured was an old, beat-up teddy bear. He always had it with him. The bear was his constant companion and friend, and offered a good shoulder to cry on. Mike and the bear were inseparable.

One day, another patient was sitting in the middle of the meeting room floor, crying. Nobody seemed to care—it was just a retarded boy, after all. Mike slowly rolled his wheelchair over to the boy. He touched him on the shoulder with his gnarled, useless hand—his version of a hug. Then he gave the boy his most prized possession; his beloved bear. Mike rolled slowly away, and the bear was gone.

Some people would call Mike a loser. But not God. God saw what Mike did. And someday Mike will be repaid for his generous love. He had little, but he gave it all. God will make it all up to him.

DISCUSSION QUESTIONS

1. **In what ways can Jesus change a life?**
2. **Why does God want us to give sacrificially?**
3. **What do you think happened to the widow after she left? Do you think she's rich in heaven? Do you think it was wise of her to give everything? How did Jesus know it was all she had? Can Jesus look into our hearts and see our motives and situations?**
4. **What are some wrong motives for giving? What are some good ones?**
5. **What sort of things can we be giving?**

Games for the klutz.

LEFTY LACERS

You need three pairs of large shoes with laces (shoes and boots can be found at thrift shops). Three volunteer couples come to the front of the group. One player from each couple removes his or her shoes. Working together as shown, couples attempt to lace the shoes. The first couple to finish is the winner. The catch is that each person in each couple can only use one hand. To make it even more difficult, require that players use their left hands (or right, if they are naturally left-handed).

LEFTOVER NAMES

If your crowd has some new faces, begin the meeting by requiring that all participants write their full names on the chalkboard or butcher paper, one person at a time, using the hand they do not normally use. Or make them write their names while looking at the reflection of the paper in a mirror—very difficult!

GRAPE SHOT

Tape a painter's paper drop cloth to the wall. Three volunteers, wearing eye protection, stand against the wall as shown. Three others use slingshots to fire grapes at the "targets," with the intention of missing the targets as closely as possible—like a knife thrower and his assistant. Allow each grape shooter to fire six grapes. When done, measure the distance between the targets and the marks the grapes left. The closest is the winner. If a volunteer intentionally hits a target, make them exchange places.

The Last Becomes First SESSION 7

INSIGHTS FOR THE LEADER

WHAT THE SESSION IS ABOUT

God exalts the humble servant.

SCRIPTURE STUDIED

Matthew 18:1-4; Mark 9:33-37; 10:35-45; Luke 18:9-14.

KEY PASSAGE

"For even the Son of Man did not come to be served, but to serve, and to give his life as a ransom for many." Mark 10:45

AIMS OF THE SESSION

During this session your learners will:

1. Compare Jesus' definition of greatness to that of the world.
2. List ways junior highers can serve others.
3. Commit themselves to an act of service.

Today's session focuses on greatness. It begins by contrasting the world's ideas of greatness—wealth, fame, success, and so on—with God's ideas. Jesus taught that the person who would be great must be a servant, that the one who would be first must be last, that the one who is humble will be exalted. Greatness in God's economy is a matter of inner attitudes which are modeled after Christ's own attitudes. This session will enable your students to explore the scriptural teachings about these attitudes and to discuss how such attitudes will manifest themselves in practical acts of service.

During the EXPLORATION part of the session your students will examine Scriptures dealing with a Christlike attitude and with Christ's teaching about the attitudes His followers should have. Junior highers can understand the ideas of not demanding one's own rights and be willing to go out of one's way to help others. They can understand the idea of obeying God instead of doing as they please, even when obedience is inconvenient or painful.

Students will take a look at a concept described in Mark 9:33-37. Christ's followers were arguing about who among them was the greatest. It's not likely that they were saying, "You're the greatest among us." "No, no, *you* are!" It was quite the reverse: "Well, I think I'm the greatest because . . . " and "Don't you remember when Jesus gave me special honor? I must be the greatest."

Junior highers can identify with this type of argument. They look for ways to be great in the eyes of others. Probably the last thing they connect with greatness is servanthood or being last. They are not far enough out of the self-centeredness of childhood to have adult ideas about putting the needs of others before their own wants and desires. But now is the time to start helping them explore these ideas.

Matthew's record of the disciples asking Jesus, "Who is the greatest?" (see Matt. 18:1-4) expands the lesson of the little child in Mark 9:36,37. Jesus taught that an attitude of humility is the key to being the greatest in the kingdom of heaven.

In a child, humility includes the ideas of teachability, dependence, trust, and love. Christians who are willing and hungry to learn about God, who trust Him rather than going it alone, and who obey Him and put Him above all else will no doubt reach great stature in God's kingdom.

The next incident also involves followers of Jesus trying to push themselves forward. James and John came to Jesus and said, "Let one of us sit at your right and the other at your left in your glory" (Mark 10:37). They were looking for secular power, quite probably, whereas Jesus came to provide a spiritual relationship with God.

NOTES

The other disciples heard about the request of James and John and were understandably indignant. So Jesus called the disciples together and told them that they must serve to be great. He said that even He came not to be served but to serve and to die in service (Mark 10:41-45).

Once again, Jesus attempted to redirect the thinking of His disciples. They needed to stop thinking in terms of their own glory and honor, and to begin thinking of how best to serve God and to bring honor to His name. They could best serve Him by serving others, following the example of their Lord. Their attitude needed to be not "What can I get from this person?" but "How can I serve this person?" This is an attitude that takes some growing into; it doesn't happen overnight, but is something God builds into junior highers or adults as they walk with Him.

In the final passage your students will study, Jesus told the parable of a Pharisee and a tax collector praying in the Temple (see Luke 18:9-14). Christ's teaching is simple to understand. In God's economy, the person who exalts himself, who thinks the world revolves around him and exists for his own benefit, is not the kind of person God will honor.

Jesus was establishing a whole new value structure. Wealth, power, success—all are nothing compared to the humble attitude of service.

This session shows that Jesus' teachings stand against the world's ideas of greatness. The attitudes that Jesus demands do not come naturally. But they do come supernaturally, to those who walk with the Lord, read their Bibles, pray, worship, and fellowship with other believers. And as the Christlike attitudes are learned, they will result in practical acts of service that your junior highers can perform.

SESSION PLAN

BEFORE CLASS BEGINS: Because there is no Compass student worksheet for this session, you will need to photocopy only the Fun Page take-home paper. See the ALTERNATE ATTENTION GRABBER and the EXPLORATION for a list of materials and pre-class preparation.

Attention Grabber

ATTENTION GRABBER (3-5 minutes)

When students are seated, say, **Everybody wants to be great at something.** Tell your students of your own personal goals when you were a young child, or the goals of some of your young friends. For example, you may have tried to be the "electronics genius" of the neighborhood, or the best Girl Scout with the most achievements, or a star Little League player.

Say, **When you were younger, what did you do that made you think you were great in the eyes of your pals? What was your claim to fame?** Allow students to respond.

Make a transition to the next part of the lesson by saying something like this: **The world has one set of ideas about what makes people great, while the Bible shows that Jesus taught a**

96

different set of ideas. We are going to see the contrast between the world's ideas and Jesus' ideas of greatness.

ALTERNATE ATTENTION GRABBER
(3-5 minutes)

Preparation: Letter the word "EMPLOYEE" on eight sheets of paper, one letter per sheet (as shown below). Do the same for the words "SLAVE" and "SERVANT."

When students are seated, write, "A person who does something for pay" on the chalkboard. Call eight students forward and give each a letter in the word "EMPLOYEE." (If you have less than eight students, give each more than one letter. An audience is not necessary.) Say, **OK, now I want you people to unscramble this word by rearranging yourselves until you are in the proper order. The word is the answer to the phrase I've written on the chalkboard.**

The audience may assist in the unscrambling. When "EMPLOYEE" is correctly spelled, congratulate volunteers and have three of them sit down. Now hand out the letters to the word "SLAVE" and ask the remaining volunteers to unscramble it. When they do, write "A person who does something because he has to" on the chalkboard. Finally, allow seven students to unscramble "SERVANT," writing "What the Bible calls someone who does something because he or she wants to" on your chalkboard.

Explain, **The Bible's notion of greatness and what makes a person great is different from the ideas many of us may have about greatness. Jesus taught that to become great in God's eyes, a person needs to be a servant to others. It's an interesting teaching, and one we will examine today.**

Bible Exploration

EXPLORATION (25-30 minutes)

Materials needed: You will need 21 sheets of construction paper (8½X11 inches is a good size), some masking tape or cellophane tape and two large sheets of butcher paper prepared as described and illustrated.

On one sheet of butcher paper, write the following verses with blank spaces. Print large, using a marker, so that all the students can read the verses from their seats.

"If _____ wants to be _____, he must be _____, and _____." Mark 9:35

"_____ wants to become _____ must be _____." Mark 10:43

"_____ did _____ to be _____, but to _____, and to _____ as a _____ for many." Mark 10:45

"_____ himself like this _____ is

NOTES

Important Note: To prevent students from recording the positions of the hidden words in the EXPLORATION activity, tell them to put away their pencils and pens.

the _____ in the _____." Matthew 18:4

"Everyone who _____ himself will be _____, and he who _____ himself will be _____." Luke 18:14

Number the sheets of construction paper 1 through 21. (You must use construction paper or some other opaque paper. Writing paper is thin enough to see through.) Tape them along their top edges to the second sheet of butcher paper, forming flaps as shown.

Under each flap, write one of the words or phrases listed below. These are the phrases that complete the Bible verses on the other butcher paper. Write the answers in random order under the flaps.

first	humbled
anyone	the Son of Man
the servant of all	not come
the very last	served
give his life	serve
child	whoever humbles
exalts	kingdom of heaven
exalted	humbles
whoever	
great among you	
your servant	
ransom	
greatest	

Before your students arrive, hang both sheets of butcher paper on the wall. Familiarize yourself with the rules of the game, which are detailed in Step 2 below.

Step 1 (3-5 minutes): To help students think about the way the world defines greatness, ask them to name several famous people and tell why they are considered great. If students need help, suggest the following categories: music heroes, movie and TV stars, political figures, rich people, scientists, and sports figures.

Say, **Thank you. But now lets look at what Jesus had to say about greatness. For although it would be nice to be famous and great in the world's eyes, we Christians know that the only truly lasting greatness is greatness in God's eyes. If He says we are great, then we are indeed great—even if the world doesn't know us at all.**

Step 2 (15-20 minutes): Now you are ready to play the game. Say, **You've noticed the papers hanging on the wall. We are going to play a simple game which will help us get a handle on what Jesus said about being great.** Tell students to follow along in their Bibles as you read Mark 9:33-35 (or ask a good reader to do so).

Now say, **The first verse on the wall is Mark 9:35. But it's full of blanks. Your job is to find the proper words to fill in the blanks. The words and phrases are hidden under the numbered flaps of paper. I will pick one of you to choose a flap, any flap. If the word or phrase is the one we are looking for, I will write it in the blank. If not, I will lower the flap and give someone else a chance. You are to refer to your Bibles so that you know what the proper words are.**

The first word your students are to find is "anyone." When someone locates it, tear the numbered flap off and use your marker to write the word on the first blank. Then begin looking for the second word, which is "first." Work on only one blank at a time, in consecutive order. Encourage your students to memorize what's under each flap as it is lifted, so that they can find it later.

When students have completed the first verse, briefly discuss its meaning and significance. Then go on to the next verse. Read Mark 10:35-45 to your students, and let them fill in the blanks of Mark 10:43 and then 10:45. The next passage to read is Matthew 18:1-4. Use material from INSIGHTS FOR THE LEADER when discussing the importance of the passage. The final passage you are to read is Luke 18:9-14.

Step 3 (5-6 minutes): When the game is completed, say, **As you can see from these verses we've studied, God's way of doing things is a lot different from the way mankind often does them. God does want to exalt us— but He will do it only if we are humble and if we serve. Let's dream up some ways to serve.**

On your chalkboard write,

HOME   CHURCH   SCHOOL   OTHER

Explain to students that you want them to brainstorm with you various ways that a junior high person could serve God by serving others. The different categories on the chalkboard are the different areas of service open to most people. As students respond, jot their answers under the appropriate headings. If students have a hard time getting started, make a few of these suggestions— HOME: clean up without complaint, do something especially nice for a family member, switch off the TV so you can actually talk to your sister. CHURCH: invite friends to activities, help set up chairs or lick envelopes, make a new kid feel welcome. SCHOOL: work hard, stay out of trouble, start an informal lunch time Bible study, give a Christian speech in English class. OTHER: help the little kid next door fix his or her bike, let an elderly person go before you in line.

Wrap up your discussion by saying something like, **We have seen that God views greatness differently than the world does. The rewards for service are great. They may come at a later date, but we have the promise of Jesus Christ—we shall be exalted someday if we serve now.**

Conclusion and Decision

CONCLUSION (1 minute)

Instruct your students to walk by the chalkboard on their way out, putting their initials on one area of service they each are willing to commit to do that week.

Your students may wish to see this solution to the Fun Page puzzle.

(If you like, write the solution on an extra copy of the Fun Page and pin it to your classroom bulletin board.)

Note: The next session requires glue, scissors, a clipboard and a copy of the Sign-Up Sheet from the "Clip Art and Other Goodies." See page 107 for details.

99

RANSOMED!

Session 7

The "HOT THOT" below indicates that Jesus gave His life to ransom us. But what does the word "ransom" literally mean? Find out fast by . . . using a dictionary. Find out SLOWLY by playing this game! It's more fun. Instructions: Notice that some of the hundreds of boxes formed by the grid lines below have gaps in their walls. Your job is to shade with a pencil those boxes that have TWO walls with gaps. Do not shade boxes with four, three, one or no gaps. This requires patience and good eyesight. The shaded boxes will spell the answer to our question. (Some boxes have been shaded as an example.)

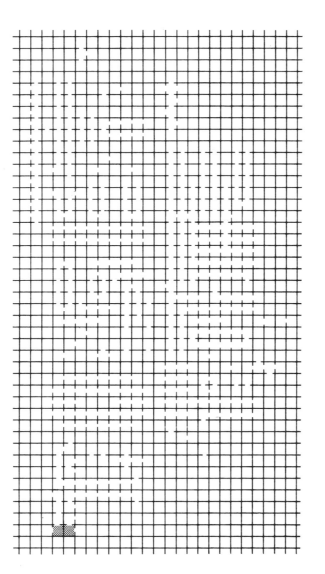

Now that you've found the answer: Jesus bought and paid for us with His life. He has cancelled any debt we owe. That is what it means to be ransomed by Jesus. He paid for our sins, He cancelled our debt. He has saved us.

© 1987 GL/LIGHT FORCE, VENTURA, CA 93006

DAILY NUGGETS Wisdom from God's Word for you to read each day.

Day 1 Read Mark 9:14-24. What did the man need in order for Jesus to heal his son?

Day 2 Mark 9:30,32. What did Jesus predict?

Day 3 Mark 9:33-37. How can we be first? In welcoming a child, who do we really welcome?

Day 4 Mark 9:31-41. What kind of reward do you think Jesus meant?

Day 5 Mark 10:1-12. Why did Moses permit divorce?

Day 6 Mark 10:13-16. In what way do you suppose we must be as children?

"For even the Son of Man did not come to be served, but to serve, and to give his life as a ransom for many."

Mark 10:45

THE COMPLETE JUNIOR HIGH BIBLE STUDY RESOURCE BOOK #2
© 1987 GL/LIGHT FORCE, VENTURA, CA 93006

THEME: God exalts the humble servant.

Session 7

BIBLE STUDY OUTLINE

Read Luke 14:7-11 to your students. Make these points as time permits:

- This passage teaches us about the key to greatness, which, as is often the case with Jesus' teachings, is completely the opposite of what the world says. The world says we must struggle to achieve and to assert ourselves. Christ says we should put others first and allow **Him** to make us great.
- Verse 7: Jesus was at a social gathering—a party. He noticed that the people were trying to establish themselves in a "pecking order." You've heard of a pecking order, haven't you? A rough, tough chicken gets to eat sooner than the weaker chickens. People are a lot like chickens; trying to be the top dog—er, bird.
- Verses 8-10: Jesus uses an illustration of a party to teach a greater truth about life—you can move up higher by putting yourself lower. That seems paradoxical, but that's the way God works it. If you want to be honored, let other people go before you.
- Verse 11: Notice that there is an outside force working to humble people who exalt themselves and exalt people who humble themselves. That force is God. He keeps careful track of the way people handle themselves, and eventually He balances the scales. He humbles the exalted and He exalts the humble. The whole secret to the matter is to walk with God and put others first. Eventually, God will reward you. Eventually, you will take your place as a major factor in the work God is doing on this planet. But you must make a habit of putting other people before you.
- Please note that to be humble does not mean to be weak and wimpy. Weak and wimpy is not what God wants. In fact, to be a truly humble Christian takes a strong personality and a determined commitment to God. To be humble means to put other people before you. And that's the secret to greatness in the kingdom of God.

"TALL TALE": THE MAN IN THE BACK SEAT

Once upon a time there was a rich, rotten old man. He treated everyone like dirt—especially the kindhearted driver, who chauffeured the mean old man in his expensive limousine. One day as the humble driver conveyed the mean old man to his summer palace, the old man said, "You're a lazy bum, driver! You should work hard, like me. Haven't you done anything with your life?"

The driver said with a smile, "I do work hard, Mr. Megabucks. And, yes, I've done something with my life: I love and serve the Lord Jesus!"

"What?!" the old man screamed. "I've been to church once or twice, but I would NEVER serve anybody."

"The Bible indicates that the first shall be last and the last shall be first," replied the driver.

"That's nonsense!" shouted the mean old man from the back seat.

At this point in the story, a giant asteroid came flying down from space, flew right at the limousine, and landed SMASH right on top of the car, squashing it as flat as a pancake. The driver and the mean old man were instantly killed.

As they floated up to heaven in a ghostly limousine, the driver said, "See what I mean, Mr. Megabucks?"

"I sure do!" he said.

You see, the driver was relaxing in splendid comfort in the back seat, and the mean old man was now driving the car.

DISCUSSION QUESTIONS

1. **Define "greatness" as the average junior high kid would define it. Define it as you think God would.**
2. **Why does God want us to put other people before ourselves? Does that mean we should allow people to take unfair advantage of us?**
3. **It sometimes seems as if this passage is wrong—that arrogant, undeserving people make it big in life while humble, nice people "bite rocks." Why? Will God eventually set things right? When?**
4. **What are some ways a person your age could put others first?**

THE COMPLETE JUNIOR HIGH
BIBLE STUDY RESOURCE
BOOK #2

Have a "Hat Night"—everyone must wear a hat to the meeting (provide a few extras for the absentminded).

HATS OFF

With everybody blindfolded, each player attempts to find his or her own hat in a pile.

HAT TOSS

Construct a ring toss game with nails and plywood (or use a hat rack)—players earn points by tossing their hats at the nails. Give each nail a different point value.

A PENNY FOR YOUR HAT

Place all hats as shown. Students attempt to toss a penny in their own hats—but must wear whichever they actually get. Have students return hats after a few minutes.

STEAL A HAT

All players assemble within a circle or square marked on the floor. At the signal, players attempt to steal hats without losing their own. Stolen hats may be tossed out of the game. When a player loses a hat, he or she must exit the game. Play continues until one player remains.

Christ Our Hope
SESSION 8

INSIGHTS FOR THE LEADER

WHAT THE SESSION IS ABOUT
Christ's predictions of our future

SCRIPTURE STUDIED
Mark 13; John 14:16,17; Romans 8:34; 1 Corinthians 10:13; 2 Timothy 3:16; 1 Peter 3:12; 5:7.

KEY PASSAGE
"At that time men will see the Son of Man coming in clouds with great power and glory." Mark 13:26

AIMS OF THE SESSION
During this session your learners will:
1. Study Christ's predictions.
2. Examine His warnings to be alert and prepared.
3. Identify His promises of protection.

Mark 13 is the biblical basis for this session. This chapter records an occasion when Jesus warned His followers about a number of upcoming difficulties, and gave them directions for responding to these events. He also spoke of his own return and urged His disciples to watch and be ready for His coming.

This session will not attempt to draw a hard, fast time line of events or reveal all hidden mysteries of the end times. Rather, it will focus primarily on one fact: Jesus is coming. Knowledge of the promised return of Christ is to be an encouragement to His followers who may be immersed in problems and difficulties in their life on earth. We know that some day we will be released from our daily struggle with our own sinful natures, with Satan's efforts to destroy us, and with the influences of the world. We look forward to enjoying fellowship with our Lord unhindered by these negative influences.

In addition to the comfort of knowing what good things lie ahead, there is great hope for the believer in simply knowing that God is in control of the world's destiny. Just as the early Christians did not panic when the Roman armies surrounded Jerusalem, believers in all times need not fear the world's catastrophes, for we have been forewarned. Wars, earthquakes, persecutions and false messiahs are no threat to Jesus' followers who see them as Jesus did: the birth pangs of the new era. Knowing how a crisis will end takes the threat away, and we know that God has already determined how He will end the struggles of human history.

The Bible
Jesus provides hope and encouragement for today through a wide variety of means available until His return. Students will look at just a few of the many ways in which He helps His people. One way is through the provision of the Word. "All Scripture is God-breathed and is useful for teaching, rebuking, correcting and training in righteousness, so that the man of God may be thoroughly equipped for every good work" (2 Tim. 3:16). The Word gives us what we need in order to live for our Lord. It teaches us about Him and what He does for us. When we are in trouble, it brings us His message of hope and comfort.

The Holy Spirit
Jesus also gives us the Holy Spirit to comfort and counsel us. He promised, "I will ask the Father, and He will give you another Counselor to be with you forever—the Spirit of truth (John 14:16,17). The Spirit helps us, strengthens us, comforts us, and teaches us about the Lord Jesus. He brings us the hope we need when we begin to get anxious about problems.

105

NOTES

hear our prayers

caring about our problems

Our Prayers

Because we know Jesus, we can be sure that God hears and answers our prayers. Peter, quoting from Psalm 34, wrote, "For the eyes of the Lord are on the righteous and his ears are attentive to their prayer" (1 Pet. 3:12). Knowing that the sovereign Lord of the universe hears our prayers and responds with the help we need gives us hope no matter what our situation.

Christ Our Defender

Students will also find that Jesus makes a defense for us. When Satan tries to bring a charge against us before the Father, "Christ Jesus . . . is at the right hand of God and is also interceding for us" (Rom. 8:34). He defends us against any accusation, because He died in order to pay the penalty of our sin. Knowing this should give believers hope and confidence in their relationship with God.

Our Worries

Jesus cares about our problems and helps us bear them. Peter wrote, "Cast all your anxiety on him because he cares for you" (1 Pet. 5:7). Instead of being anxious and worried, Christians can have hope because the Lord helps them with their problems.

Our Escape

protects against temptation

Finally, our Lord protects us when we are tempted and helps us not to sin. Scripture promises, "No temptation has seized you except what is common to man. And God is faithful; he will not let you be tempted beyond what you can bear. But when you are tempted, he will also provide a way out so that you can stand up under it" (1 Cor. 10:13). He knows our weaknesses and He does not expect us to bear more than we are able. Christians can have hope, when facing temptation, that God will not let the temptation become more than they can bear, or else He will provide an escape.

As you guide your students through this session, stress the hope that believers find in Jesus. Make sure students clearly understand that this hope is available only to those who know Jesus personally. It is significant that Jesus concluded His discourse with repeated emphasis on being alert, living with the assurance that Jesus will return suddenly, at a time known only to the Father. This alertness is similar to that of an athlete who stays in condition to be ready for any challenge that might come. Jesus calls His followers to be awake, ready to welcome His return. Make yourself available to talk individually with students who may need further counseling about their personal readiness for His coming.

- we have hope when facing temptation only to those who know Jesus

SESSION PLAN

BEFORE CLASS BEGINS: Unless you have more than about 12 students, you will need to do no photocopying before class, except the Fun Page. If you have more students, you should make extra copies of the Teacher's Resource pages. There is no Compass worksheet for this session. Materials required are scissors and glue for each of three groups of learners. (More groups should be formed if you have over 12 or so students.) You will also need a clipboard and the sign-up sheet from the "Clip Art and Other Goodies" section at the back of this book.

Attention Grabber

ATTENTION GRABBER (2-3 minutes)

When students have taken their seats, say, **I want you to suggest several ways that people try to predict the future, or the things they use to try to predict the future.** (Some things are crystal balls, Ouija boards, fortune cookies, astrology, and palm readers.)

Say, **People at racetracks lose a lot of money betting on horses they feel will win. They are hoping they've accurately predicted the future.**

A lot of people worry about the future, not knowing what to expect, hoping it won't be bad. But Jesus told His disciples many interesting things about the future, about *our* future, and today we are going to take a look at what we can expect to see in the final days of the world we now know.

Bible Exploration

EXPLORATION (30-40 minutes)

Materials needed: The three Teacher's Resource pages for this session, three scissors, and three bottles of glue or paste. (You will need to double up on these materials if you have more than 12-15 students. If you do, photocopy an extra set of Teacher's Resource pages for every additional 15 students.) You also need a clipboard and the sign-up sheet from the "Clip Art and Other Goodies" section.

Step 1 (5-6 minutes): Assemble students into

If you can stand to handle one, you might bring in a "stars predict the coming year" horoscope magazine to show your students to what silly lengths people go to know the future.

NOTES

three groups of three to five students each. If you have too many students, form an extra three groups, no group having less than two students. (If you have a very small class, allow students to work on the following assignments individually.)

Read all of Mark 13 aloud to your students as they follow along in their Bibles (or allow several volunteers to read portions).

Finally, distribute the Teacher's Resource pages, one page per group. Notice that the pages are labeled "Group 1," "Group 2," and "Group 3."

Step 2 (15-20 minutes): Explain, **We are going to make a book. It is called "The Christian's Survival Manual," and it is about the things that Jesus said will happen in the future, what we should do to prepare ourselves for that future, and God's promises that we can count on to get us through that future.**

There are three sections to our manual. Each group has one section to work on. On the sheet you have been given are instructions on what to do. Notice that you have some cartoon art to cut and paste, and some blanks to fill in. It's easy to do and if you have any

questions I'll come around to help.

When we are all through, we will discuss some of the things Jesus said. At the end of class I will gather your sections of the manual. Later, I will make photocopies and assemble enough books for all of you to have. Then I'll mail you each a copy to keep. I want you to have fun in your groups, but remember that this is a serious topic and I want you to put your best efforts into this project. Now I want you to read the instructions on your pages.

Distribute scissors and glue. Walk around to observe students' progress. Encourage all students to be involved in their group's efforts. As students work, have them pass around and sign the sign-up sheet on the clipboard.

Step 3 (10-15 minutes): When groups have completed their individual sections of the manual, they are to share what they've written with the other students. Lead a discussion on the significance of what they have learned. Be sure to go over the additional Bible passages that students glued to their pages (use INSIGHTS FOR THE LEADER).

Conclusion and Decision

CONCLUSION (3-5 minutes)

Instruct students to individually choose the statement Jesus made that means the most to them. Say, **Rewrite the statement in your own words on a blank sheet of paper. Fold the paper into your Bible as a reminder of Christ's promises for the future.**

Collect the students' manuals and *be sure* all

students have signed their names and addresses on the clipboard.

Close in prayer and distribute the Fun Page.

As soon as possible, make copies of the Survival Manuals, bind them with staples, put stamps and addresses on them and drop them in the mail.

Note: The next session, session 9, requires balloons, marshmallows, flour, cookies, punch and a couple of other things. See page 120 for details.

The Official
CHRISTIAN'S SURVIVAL MANUAL

Published by the Kids at

Group 1 INSTRUCTIONS:

1. Cut this page into two pieces along the dotted line.

2. Working together in your group, answer all the questions on the other piece. Fill in all the blanks.

3. When you have answered the questions, use your scissors to clip out the cartoons below. (Clip along the dotted lines.) Glue the cartoons to the spots you think are best, next to the questions you have answered. Clip out and glue the "Definition of an Abomination" to its proper place. Use the "Cover Clip Art" to create a nice cover design.

Cover Clip Art

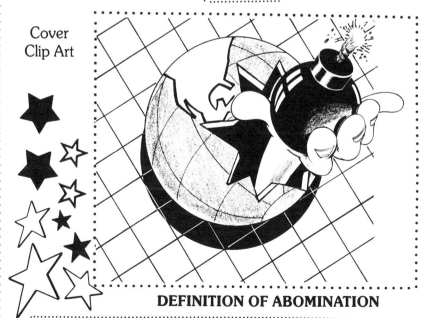

DEFINITION OF ABOMINATION

Nobody knows for sure, but the "abomination that causes desolation" is apparently some symbol of evil that Satan causes to be placed in the Temple. It may be an evil person who will come in the future (see 2 Thessalonians 2:3,4).

WHAT ON EARTH'S GOING TO HAPPEN?
Read Mark 13

Introduction: This Survival Manual shows what Jesus said would happen in the future (some has already happened); what we Christians should do to prepare ourselves, and some comforting promises that Jesus made.

13:1-2 The stones in the Temple in Jerusalem will be _____.

13:5-8
Many will come _____.

You will hear of _____.

Nation and kingdom will _____.

In various places there will be _____.

13:9-13
You will be _____.

On account of Jesus you _____.

You will be arrested and _____.

But just say _____.

Brother will _____.

Father will _____.

Children will _____.

All men will _____.

13:14-21 Summarize this passage in a couple of sentences.

Definition of Abomination

13:22-26
False _____
_____.

The sun and moon will _____.

The Son of Man will _____.

Angels will _____.

WHAT SHOULD WE DO? (MARK 13)

		Place cartoons and verses in this column.
13:5	Watch out for what?	
13:7	Do not be what?	
13:9	You must be what?	
13:11	Don't worry about what?	
	Just say what?	
	Because why?	

Sum up what we are told to do in verses 14-19 in a sentence or two:

Page 2

Group 2 INSTRUCTIONS:

1. **Cut this page into two pieces along the dotted line.**
2. **Working together in your group, answer all the questions on the other piece.**
3. **When you have answered the questions, use your scissors to clip out the cartoons below. (Clip along the dotted lines.) Glue the cartoons to the spots you think are best, next to the questions you have answered. Clip out the Bible verses below and glue them by the questions to which you think they apply.**

"Cast all your anxiety on him because he cares for you."
1 Peter 5:7

"For the eyes of the Lord are on the righteous and his ears are attentive to their prayer."
1 Peter 3:12

"Christ Jesus, who died—more than that, who was raised to life—is at the right hand of God and is also interceding for us."
Romans 8:34

13:21   Don't believe what?

13:22   Why shouldn't we believe it?

13:23   Be on what?

13:28   Learn what lesson?

Explain.

13:35   Therefore, keep what?

Why?

13:37   What does Jesus say?

JESUS' PROMISES (MARK 13)

Things Jesus said that give us comfort.

13:11 It's the Holy Spirit who will _____

_____.

13:13 He who stands firm to the end will _____

_____.

13:20 What will the Lord do for the elect?

13:26 Men will see _____

_____.

13:27 His angels will _____

_____.

13:31 What never passes away (or fails)?

Group 3 INSTRUCTIONS:

1. Cut this page into two pieces along the dotted line.

2. Working together in your group, answer all the questions on the other piece. Fill in all the blanks.

3. When you have answered all the questions, use your scissors to clip out the cartoons below. (Clip along the dotted lines.) Glue the cartoons to the spots you think are best, next to the questions you have answered. Clip out the Bible verses below and glue them by the questions to which you think they apply.

"And I will ask the Father, and he will give you another Counselor to be with you forever— the Spirit of truth."
John 14:16,17

"And God is faithful; he will not let you be tempted beyond what you can bear."
1 Corinthians 10:13

"All Scripture is God-breathed and is useful for teaching, rebuking, correcting and training in righteousness, so that the man of God may be thoroughly equipped for every good work."
2 Timothy 3:16

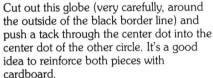

DISAPPEARING CHRISTIAN!

"For the Lord himself will come down from heaven, with a loud command, with the voice of the archangel and with the trumpet call of God, and the dead in Christ will rise first. After that, we who are still alive and are left will be caught up together with them in the clouds to meet the Lord in the air. And so we will be with the Lord forever." 1 Thessalonians 4:16,17

Here's a very strange puzzler to help illustrate the Christians' resurrection. Put it together and try it on your friends. See how many of them can explain how or why it works!

Cut out this globe (very carefully, around the outside of the black border line) and push a tack through the center dot into the center dot of the other circle. It's a good idea to reinforce both pieces with cardboard.

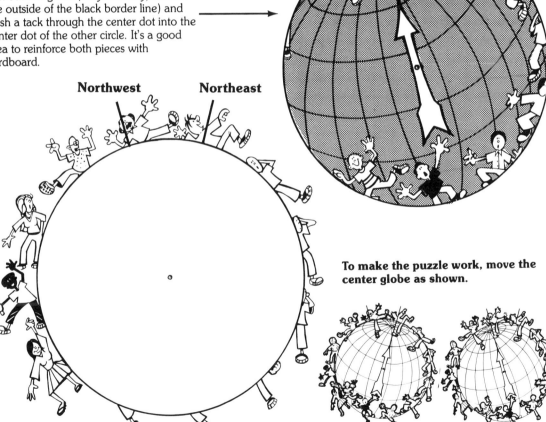

Northwest   **Northeast**

To make the puzzle work, move the center globe as shown.

COUNT THE PEOPLE! When the arrow points to the Northeast, there are 13 people. But when it points to the Northwest, there are only 12! Which person vanished? Where did he go?

DAILY NUGGETS

Day 1 Read Mark 10:17-27. What one thing did the man lack?

Day 2 Mark 10:28-31. When we leave everything to follow Jesus, what is our reward?

Day 3 Mark 10:32-34. What did Jesus tell the twelve about coming events in Jerusalem?

Day 4 Mark 10: 41-45. How do we become great?

Day 5 Mark 10:46-52. Is there something you can ask Jesus for in faith?

Day 6 Mark 11:1-10. How would you like to welcome Jesus if He came to your town?

"At that time men will see the Son of Man coming in clouds with great power and glory."

Mark 13:26

THE COMPLETE JUNIOR HIGH BIBLE STUDY RESOURCE BOOK #2
© 1987 GL/LIGHT FORCE, VENTURA, CA 93006

THEME: The coming of the Lord.

Session 8

BIBLE STUDY OUTLINE

This study is based on 1 Thessalonians 4:13-5:6. As you go over it with your listeners, make the following points as time allows:

- Verse 13: Evidently some of Paul's readers thought that Jesus intended to return before any Christian died. When some did die, the Thessalonians were confused, so Paul wrote this part of the letter. "Fall asleep" means to die, and conveys the fact that, for the Christian, death is not a final, hopeless situation. It is like sleep from which we awake.
- Psalm 116:15 tells us, "Precious in the sight of the Lord is the death of his saints." God takes great interest in our final moments on this planet. When Paul says we are not to grieve, he did not mean we couldn't feel sorrow for the loss of a friend or loved one. He meant that we needn't grieve with the hopeless, never-to-return concept of death the pagan nonbelievers had.
- I Thessalonians 4:14-17: Because Jesus took our death upon Himself, and because He rose, we can look forward to being raised. We who are alive will be caught up in the air, and we will be with the Lord forever. In order to be with the Lord then, we need to be with Him now—by being dedicated disciples of Christ.
- Verse 18: We are to encourage each other with this information. I hope you find this resurrection an exciting prospect—it's going to be a wild experience!
- Verses 5:1-3: The day when this all happens will come like a thief in the night—unpredictably, without warning, and with disastrous results for those who are not prepared (non-Christians). There is no second chance for the unprepared. We won't be able to say, "Oops! Wait a minute, Jesus—let me get right with you!"
- Verses 4-6: Paul contrasts the spiritual light that Christians enjoy to the evil darkness that nonbelievers dwell in. While Paul was still a hater of Jesus and His disciples, Jesus appeared to him and said, "I am sending you to them (nonbelievers) to open their eyes and turn them from darkness to light, and from the power of Satan to God" (see Acts 26:17,18). We are of God, and Jesus will one day come to take us home. Finally, Paul warns us to stay alert and self-controlled. We are not to be drowsy or sleepy. We are not to slip into sin or stray from God's side (see 1 Thess. 5:6). Not because we will miss the day of the Lord, but because we won't be very good servants here on earth.

TRUE STORY: A CHRISTIAN GOES HOME

Jana had just been told she had cancer. Her doctors wanted to operate within the week. What an experience for a popular ninth-grade cheerleader! Cancer. Didn't cancer happen to old people—not vibrant, active 14-year-old girls?

Jana and her family were active at church. They called the minister for comfort and advice. When he heard the story, he said there was no real option but to operate.

The operation brought more bad news. The doctors said the cancer was so advanced she only had six months to live. She would soon have to be medicated to endure the pain.

Jana remained strong in her faith. But her parents' faith wavered. They were bitter and angry at God. Some of Jana's friends in the youth group would come over every day and pray with her. The pain increased. Her faith remained strong while her parents' faith deteriorated. Jana was actually an inspiration to her friends.

Six months from the day of her operation, Jana died. There were over 1,000 people at her funeral. It was the saddest day for those who knew her. Yet Jana's short life had been an inspiration. Along with grief, her friends experienced a certain amount of deeply-rooted joy and peace. Jana no longer lived in pain. She was with the Lord Jesus whom she loved so much.

Her parents never set foot in a church again.

DISCUSSION QUESTIONS

1. **If a Christian friend of yours had to face death, would you try to understand God's reasons, or be bitter with Him? What would you say to Jana's parents to help their hurt?**
2. **Have you ever heard someone say, "I'll become a Christian when I'm 94 years old and on my deathbed"? Why is this a foolish thing to say? How would you respond to someone who said this to you?**
3. **What would you do if you learned Jesus was coming back in exactly one week?**
4. **What would you do if He was going to come back in exactly 25 years?**
5. **The Thessalonians obviously thought He was going to return any day. Why do you suppose He didn't?**

It's OK to play with your food.

RELAY PIES

This is a glorified pie-eating contest. Make whipped cream pies, each containing a folded index card or other relatively easy-to-pick-up object (pick up with the mouth, that is). You will need one pie for each player, or someone to refill each pie tin with whipped cream and index cards as players run back and forth.

The first player from each team runs to the pie, digs in without hands, grabs the card or other object (with his or her mouth), runs back and tags the next player who then repeats the cycle. The object is discarded. First team to go through all pies wins.

WATERMELON FACE

Obtain large watermelons. Students carve masks, which they then wear for a "beauty" contest. Judges decide the winner. If watermelons are not large enough to wear whole, split them in two and allow students to hold them up to their faces. Provide washcloths and water for clean up.

MARSHMALLOW SPIT

By spitting marshmallows out of their mouths, students attempt to make a "basket" in a bowl. The bowl should be about three or four feet away. Give each player three chances.

MARSHMALLOW TOSS

Stand one player on a chair, holding a bowl as shown. A player partner, standing several yards away, tries to score a "basket." The player on the chair may move the bowl to try to catch the marshmallow, but he or she may never leave the chair. Give each couple ten marshmallows. Couple with the highest total score wins.

Giving Our Lives to God SESSION 9

WHAT THE SESSION IS ABOUT

The most valuable gift one can give to God is one's life.

SCRIPTURE STUDIED

Matthew 22:37; Mark 14:1-9; Romans 12:1; Galatians 5:22,23.

KEY PASSAGE

"Therefore, I urge you, brothers, in view of God's mercy, to offer your bodies as living sacrifices, holy and pleasing to God—this is your spiritual act of worship." Romans 12:1

AIMS OF THE SESSION

During this session your learners will:
1. Examine the account of a woman who gave Christ a valuable gift.
2. Determine that one's life is the best gift to give to God.
3. Express their willingness to give their lives to God.

INSIGHTS FOR THE LEADER

In this session your students will examine the incident in which a woman broke a jar of expensive perfume and poured it on Jesus' head. This incident is recorded in Mark 14:1-9. It took place a few days before the Crucifixion, at a time when the chief priests were plotting how to arrest and kill Him. Jesus was in Bethany, on the outskirts of Jerusalem, eating a meal in the home of a man known as Simon the Leper. According to the account in John 12, Lazarus was there, as were his sisters, Mary and Martha. While Martha assisted with the serving, Mary anointed Jesus with the perfume.

A Beautiful Thing

The perfume was expensive, worth about a year's wages for an ordinary worker. Some of the disciples objected to this "waste" of a valuable item. John says it was Judas who said something about it. Judas pretended to be concerned for the poor, to whom the money could have been given if the perfume had been sold. But he was really concerned about his own profit. According to John, Judas kept the money for the group and "used to help himself to what was put into" the money bag (see John 12:6). Jesus rebuked those who scolded Mary for "wasting" the perfume. "Leave her alone," He said. "Why are you bothering her? She has done a beautiful thing to me. The poor you will always have with you, and you can help them any time you want. But you will not always have me. She did what she could. She poured perfume on my body beforehand to prepare for my burial" (Mark 14:6-8).

Mary was expressing her love and devotion to Jesus. She appreciated His ministry, and she wanted to return something to Him. She wanted to give a gift of great value. Whether she realized it or not, she was preparing His body for burial. The custom of the day was to anoint a body with oils in preparation for burial—this was not done for executed criminals. Jesus knew that His execution was imminent, and He had been telling His disciples that it was so. Perhaps Mary realized that this might be her last chance to love Him in a concrete way.

It is evident that Jesus, in turn, appreciated Mary's act of kindness. Although Jesus was facing the loneliness and agony of the cross courageously, He dreaded it all the same, as demonstrated by His prayer vigil at Gethsemane. Mary's loving deed must have meant a great deal to Him as He went through those last days.

Believers today have the advantage of looking back to the cross instead of ahead. We can understand more fully than Mary could what Christ has done for us. We know the price He paid for us. We have all the more reason to give Him gifts.

NOTES

A Gift Your Students Can Give

The goal of this session is to encourage your students to think of a gift that they can give God—something that He would appreciate and that He would not have otherwise. This gift is their love, their lives, their hearts and souls and minds (see Matthew 22:37) to use as He sees fit. Paul urged believers "to offer your bodies as living sacrifices, holy and pleasing to God" (Rom. 12:1). This gift of oneself means allowing God's Word to set the standard for our behavior, His Spirit to tame our natural impulses, and Jesus' life to be the model that we attempt to follow.

This gift is something that believers need to be continually giving. We can do it at one point, but it is all too easy to take back the control of our lives. We need to repeat or reaffirm the gift day by day.

What will Christ do with those who give themselves to Him? He will mold them and develop them to become more like Him. He will cause them to become fruitful with love, joy, peace, patience, kindness and the other spiritual fruit of God (see Gal. 5:22,23). He will satisfy the desires of their hearts (see Ps. 37:4)—often by changing those desires into something that honors Him more.

Like the woman with the perfume, each junior high student has a beautiful and valuable gift to offer to Jesus. That gift is the gift of their love, their aspirations, their energy, their ambitions—their lives. Encourage your students to respond to Jesus' great love by offering Him their love in return.

SESSION PLAN

BEFORE CLASS BEGINS: To help your students learn and retain the idea of giving their lives as gifts to God, this session will be a party with games and refreshments. Preparation is easy, but there are a few special materials to supply. See the ATTENTION GRABBER and EXPLORATION. Also, unlike the last few times, there is a Compass student worksheet to photocopy.

Attention Grabber

ATTENTION GRABBER (5-6 minutes)

Materials needed: Party balloons—one for each student, felt markers, and masking tape.

When students have been seated, say, **We are about to take a look at Mark 14:1-9, which is the story of a woman who gave a very expensive present to Jesus. Because we are going to be talking about gifts and giving gifts, I thought it would be nice to have a little party of our own today. I brought balloons, party games and some refreshments. Jesus is our guest of honor, so let's party!**

Hand out the balloons, one per student. Tell your listeners that they are to each think of the one thing for which they are most thankful to God. When they decide, they are to use the markers to write that thing (one or two words) on the uninflated balloons. They then inflate the balloons, tie them tight and tape them in a bunch to the wall as a decoration. To help students think of things they are thankful for, you might suggest health, friends, and so on. (Be prepared to help some students tie their balloons.)

Bible Exploration

EXPLORATION (30-40 minutes)

Materials needed: Refreshments. (Don't go to a lot of trouble. Store-bought cookies and punch are fine.) Marshmallows, a pan of white flour (to roll the marshmallows in), and butcher paper. Push some tables together so students can work and enjoy the refreshments together. Optional: small game prizes such as candy bars.

Step 1 (5-6 minutes): Create a party atmosphere by having the class circle their chairs about the tables. Place the refreshments within reach (or have a couple of volunteers help).

Say, **We are celebrating Jesus because of all the great things He has given us.** Read some of the things students have written on the balloons. Suggest other things also, if you see fit.

Before we play some party games, I want to read Mark 14:1-9 to you, and then we'll have a prayer of thanks for the food.

Read the passage to your students as they follow along in their Bibles (or have volunteers read). Lead a prayer of thanks.

Step 2 (20-30 minutes) The following three party games will help your students examine what the Bible says about today's subject, and to see how it applies to their own lives. The games will be played one at a time by the entire class, but if you have a very large number of students, you should assemble into two or more groups with other leaders, preferably in other rooms.

GAME ONE: MARSHMALLOW DARTS

Put a sheet of butcher paper on the table. The paper should be a square at least two feet wide. Tell students to draw a target on the sheet, a target with at least four rings (as shown). Explain, **I want you**

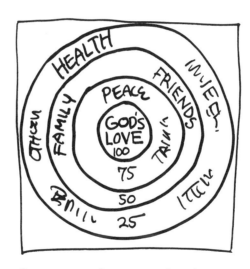

to each write on the target the thing you wrote on your balloon, or anything else you have thought of. In other words, fill the target with great things God has done for us. But leave the bull's eye blank: I want one of you to write "God's Love" in the bull's eye. Using your marker, assign points to each ring, as in the illustration. Be sure students understand that the gifts themselves aren't particularly worth more or less, just the rings.

121

NOTES

Tape the target to a convenient wall. Place a piece of tape on the floor about ten feet from the target. The tape is the foul line. Line students up single file behind the foul line. Each player gets three chances to hit the target with a marshmallow. Roll the marshmallow in flour so that the spot where the marshmallow hit can be seen. Add up each player's score on the chalkboard. (You may wish to offer a small prize to each winner of the games.)

When the game is over, say something like, **Great job! Now, this silly dart game had an important point. These things on the dart board target are some of the gifts that God has given us because of His great love. We are now going to play a simple game you've all played before. But this time the game will be about the one gift that God wants from you and me.**

GAME TWO: HANGMAN

Your students are to guess six words. The first word is "heart." On your chalkboard, draw five blanks to represent the five letters of "heart."

Say, **We are going to play "Hangman." Your job is to guess six words. As you can see on the chalkboard, the first word has five letters. I'm going to go around the table, allowing you to each have one guess at a letter. Of course, if you guess a correct letter, I will write it on the proper blank. If you don't guess correctly, I'll give the next person a chance. When one of you thinks you can guess the word, raise your hand and I will call on you.**

When someone identifies the word, draw four blanks on the chalkboard and allow students to guess the next word, which is "soul." The third word is "mind." (If time appears to be running short, you can list all three words—in blanks—at one time and put the proper letters in all three as students make their guesses.)

After the three words have been identified, tell students to turn in their Bibles to Matthew 22:36-38. Read the passage aloud. Explain, **This is the one gift that God wants from you and me:**

ourselves. **He wants us to love Him heart, soul and mind. Nothing else is really of that much value to Him. He wants us. To prove that this is so, we'll guess three more words. These are harder to guess.**

The next three words are from Romans 12:1— "bodies," "living," and "sacrifices." Because this is a famous passage, some of your students might have it memorized and thus be able to guess the third word after doing the first two. We suggest you do "living" first, then "bodies" and "sacrifices." The first two require six blanks each, "sacrifices" requires ten.

After the students have identified the words, read Romans 12:1 and say, **This verse simply means that we are to give our lives completely to God. To put Him first before all else. That is the greatest gift you can give your Lord.**

Well, we have one game left. I thought we would play a game that shows just a few of the things that God gives to us when we give our lives to Him. These are great gifts and ones that He does promise to give to those who are His.

GAME THREE: SCRAMBLED WORDS

As you write the following scrambled words on the board, inform students that they are to grab pen and paper and work individually on the words. First one done is the winner. (A few students may realize that these are the words of Galatians 5:22,23. That's OK, one of them will win.) Have the first one through read the answers. If you have too much time left, let many of the students finish before someone reads the answers.

(The words have been placed in random order to help prevent students recognizing the passage too quickly.)

TECNPAIE	AEECP
EEEGNNSTSL	SINKEDSN
OLEV	AUEFFHSSLITN
DSSOOGNE	CF-LESOONTRL
YJO	

Read and discuss Galatians 5:22,23. Remind students that these are just some of the many wonderful gifts God grants to those who are His.

Step 3 (3-5 minutes): Sum up what has just been learned during the course of the session, and lead a discussion about practical ways junior high students can give heart, soul and mind to God. Suggested responses are: becoming a Christian in the first place, obeying what is read in the Bible, asking God to make them the persons He wants them to be, spending a good amount of time in prayer and fellowship, and various acts of service.

Conclusion and Decision

CONCLUSION (3-5 minutes)

Distribute the Compass student worksheets and tell students, **These are "invitations" that you are going to fill out. They are invitations that God is sending to you for the greatest party ever. In the blank that says, "Bring a gift," write the one gift you think God would want you to give Him. If you've been paying attention today, you already know what gift God wants. Then, check one of the little boxes, whichever one truly expresses how you feel. Keep the invitation as a reminder of the big party that we call heaven.**

Close in prayer and distribute the Fun Page. Ask volunteers to help pick up the room.

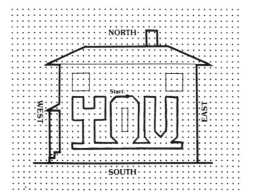

Your students may wish to see this solution to the Fun Page puzzle.

(If you like, write the solution on an extra copy of the Fun Page and pin it to your classroom bulletin board.)

Note: See the note on page 133, and "BEFORE CLASS BEGINS" on page 132.

COMPASS

YOU'RE INVITED!

To the Party to End All Parties: Eternal Life in Heaven!

Come as you are
(God will make you what He wants you to be).

Bring a gift: _____

☐ I'll bring this gift!
☐ I may give God the gift later.
☐ I'm not interested in giving God this gift.

MAP IT OUT!

Session 9

Let's say you're one of the Wise Men, you've just heard that Jesus is born, and you want to bring Him a gift. But what? You madly search all over your house to find something. We've designed this little game to help you seek and find the thing in your house you should give to Jesus. Here's how to play: Place the point of your pencil on the "Start" dot on the map below. Connect the proper dots by following the instructions on the "House Guide." Your path will lead you to the proper answer. (If you mess up, your teacher has the solution.)

House Guide

Follow each step. Draw your line:

2 dots west (This has been done on the map as an example.)
1 dot southwest (Also done as an example.)
6 dots south
1 southeast
4 west
4 north
2 east
4 north
2 west
2 south
2 west
2 north
2 west
4 south
2 east
4 south
2 west
1 south
20 east
1 north
2 west
1 northeast
7 north
2 west
6 south
1 southwest
1 northwest
6 north
2 west
7 south
1 southeast
3 west
1 northeast
6 north
1 northwest
1 west

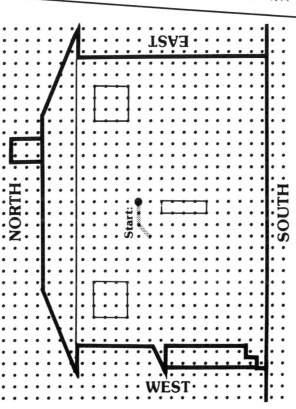

NORTH
EAST
Start:
SOUTH
WEST

Now you know what to give. At least you do if you take a close look at the path you made. Remember, God loves you just the way you are. Don't worry if you think the gift isn't good enough. It's just what He wants.

© 1987 GL/LIGHT FORCE, VENTURA, CA 93006

DAILY NUGGETS Wisdom from God's Word for you to read each day.

Day 1 Read Mark 11:22-24. What must we do in order to receive what we ask in prayer?

Day 2 Mark 11:25. Is there someone you need to forgive?

Day 3 Mark 11:28-33. Why couldn't the chief priests and teachers answer Jesus' question?

Day 4 Mark 12:13-17. How did Jesus get out of the trap?

Day 5 Mark 12:18-27. Jesus accused these people of not knowing what?

Day 6 Mark 12:28-33. What are the two most important commandments?

"Therefore, I urge you, brothers, in view of God's mercy, to offer your bodies as living sacrifices, holy and pleasing to God—which is your spiritual worship."
Romans 12:1

THEME: Giving yourself to God.

Session 9

BIBLE STUDY OUTLINE

Read Luke 9:57-62 to your students. Make these points as time allows:

- Jesus was traveling toward Jerusalem (see 9:51), soon to meet His death on the cross. With Him were His close disciples, and probably quite a few hangers-on. One said, "I will follow you wherever you go" (v. 57). It sounded noble. The guy was probably all charged up emotionally. He had probably heard Jesus teach amazing things and work incredible miracles. So on an impulse, he blurted out this pledge of commitment. But Jesus did not need any fair-weather friends. He told the man in no uncertain terms that they would not be staying in the Jerusalem Hilton. The kind of life Jesus calls us to lead can be a real test of our commitment. It is not always easy to follow Christ. Some of you may have learned this already. You may have seen friends "bomb out" on God.

- Jesus then asked another man to follow Him (v. 59). But the man wanted to bury his father. A reasonable request, if his father was dead. (He may have meant, "Let me stay at home until my father dies of old age!") But even reasonable requests are no excuse for not following Jesus. If you wish to give your life to God, you'd better plan on doing what He tells you—even if it means giving up things you don't want to give up and going places you don't want to go. Jesus replied that the spiritually dead could make themselves useful burying the physically dead. The spiritually alive should be out spreading the news of spiritual life. If you are a Christian, you are spiritually alive. Even if you are a brand-new Christian, you can be of value to God. He will use you, at whatever level you are qualified—but only if you do what He says. No excuses.

- In verse 61, someone said, "First let me go back and say good-by to my family." Now that **has** to be a reasonable request, but again, when Jesus says jump, you must say, "When can I come down?" And don't forget, Jesus only had a very short time before His death. If the man had gone home to say good-by to his family, he wouldn't have been around to say good-by to Christ. He would have missed everything. Disciples are supposed to be in the center of what God is doing, not off down the road. I hope you are interested in following God. If you are, remember to listen to Christ and to obey Him always. And heed what Jesus said in verse 62: "No one who puts his hand to the plow and looks back is fit for service in the kingdom of God." Don't look back or turn away from God. He'll guide you. Just follow Him.

OBJECT LESSON: THE JUNK TRUNK

Bring an empty suitcase to show your students. Say, **Pretend Jesus suddenly informed you that you were to hit the road on a long journey, and that you could only take what you could carry in this case. Think of all the possessions you have, especially the prized ones. Now decide what you would take.**

Give some examples of the sort of things kids tend to own (bikes, beds, clothes, skateboards, pets, books, hobby things, TV sets, stereos and the like). Ask your listeners what they would put in the suitcase. Ask them if they would be willing to leave everything they have to follow Jesus. Point out that Jesus is looking for disciples who aren't tied down by their possessions and interests.

DISCUSSION QUESTIONS

1. **What are some things that make it hard to be a Christian at home?**
2. **What makes it hard to be a Christian at school?**
3. **Read Matthew 22:36,37, about the greatest commandment. How does this commandment relate to what Christ said in Luke 9:57-62?**
4. **Have any of you ever sensed God calling you to a deeper commitment to Him? What was your response? How does your response affect your daily life?**

THE COMPLETE JUNIOR HIGH
BIBLE STUDY RESOURCE
BOOK #2

**You'll want to take pictures of
this first game.**

STEAL THE ANIMAL

Assemble two teams on two sides of a square. Line up players according to size, and number them as illustrated (lightweight matched with lightweight, and so on). Two lightweight volunteers (males) are placed in the center of the square, each player representing his team.

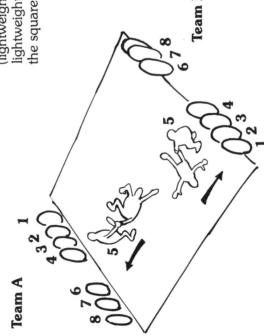

Team A

Team B

The leader calls out a number at random, such as five. The number five players run into the square, grab the opposite team's representative and attempt to pull him to the sideline (see illustration). The first representative to completely cross the line loses the round. Use a line judge at each side to decide winners. The representatives do everything in their power to avoid crossing the line first. They may attempt to hold on to the other representative or other players in the square. If the smaller players have too tough a time pulling the representatives, call an additional number to assist them.

This is a rugged game, so caution players to avoid unnecessary roughness.

A MINUTE OF SILENCE

When students are quietly seated, waiting for announcements or for whatever reason, tell them you are going to play a guessing game. At the signal, they are to silently count seconds until they think one minute has gone by. As each student thinks time is up, he or she silently raises a hand. After all hands are raised, reveal who made the closest guess. There may be ties. Naturally, you will need a watch with a second hand and students must be warned not to look at their own watches. Be sure they cannot see a clock on the wall.

To make things a little tougher, sing a song while students count.

His Death

WHAT THE SESSION IS ABOUT

The Crucifixion.

SCRIPTURE STUDIED

Mark 11:15-18; 14:1,2; 15; 15:1-47; John 5:8,9,16-18; 10:17,18; 11:49-53; Romans 3:23; 5:8; 1 Corinthians 15:3; 1 Peter 2:24.

KEY PASSAGE

"He himself bore our sins in his body on the tree, so that we might die to sins and live for righteousness; by his wounds you have been healed." 1 Peter 2:24

AIMS OF THE SESSION

During this session your learners will:

1. Study the account of the crucifixion in Mark 15.
2. Understand that Christ died for each person's sins.
3. Evaluate their own relationship to Christ.

INSIGHTS FOR THE LEADER

This session focuses on Jesus' death by crucifixion. You and your students will conduct a mock trial to determine who was responsible for His death. The answer is that all people of all times are guilty, for Christ died for the whole world (see 1 Cor. 15:3; 1 John 2:2). Your students will act as witnesses at the trial, reading many passages of Scripture that will cause them to have a good understanding of what happened and why.

The main passage is Mark 15. The chapter begins with the chief priests, the elders, the teachers of the law, and the whole Sanhedrin deciding to hand Jesus over to Pilate. This decision followed the night during which Jesus was arrested and brought before the Sanhedrin for trial (see Mark 14). If you have a lot of class time, you may wish to read Mark 14 to your students before the lesson begins.

The Sanhedrin was a body of Jewish leaders who performed the functions of a court. They had jurisdiction over civil and criminal matters. In Jewish law they were granted the power of capital punishment, but the Roman system required the Sanhedrin to go to the Roman procurator for confirmation of death sentences. This confirmation was usually granted.

Chapter 15 of Mark describes Pilate's efforts to free Jesus, which failed because of the mob's demands for crucifixion. The soldiers then mocked Jesus and took Him to His place of crucifixion.

His death was witnessed by many, including a centurion who exclaimed, "Surely this man was the Son of God!" (v. 39). Finally, Joseph of Arimathea took Christ's body and laid it in a tomb while the two women named Mary looked on.

The Verdict

Your learners will hear the testimonies of many people who plotted Jesus' death, including the chief priests, the Jewish leaders, Caiaphas, and some teachers of the law. But it is the final witness, the apostle Paul, who will reveal that the actual people responsible for His crucifixion are the sinners—every man, woman, and child who ever lived or ever will live.

First Corinthians 15:3 makes it clear that "Christ died for our sins according to the Scriptures." Romans 5:8 says, "But God demonstrates his own love for us in this: While we were still sinners, Christ died for us." And Romans 3:23 tells us that "all have sinned and fall short of the glory of God." We are all sinners and Jesus died because of our sins. We therefore are responsible for His death.

In the final moments of the session, students will read 1 Peter 2:24: "He himself bore our sins in his body on the tree, so that we might die to sins and live for righteousness; by his wounds you have been healed." (Peter

used the word "tree" for the cross because in the Old Testament days, hated people were killed and their bodies hung on trees. Thus, Peter points to the utter shame Jesus endured so that we could be saved.)

Jesus came to provide eternal life. In order to accomplish that purpose, He had to die, so He allowed Himself to be crucified (see John 10:17,18). Since his enemies conspired to kill Him for their own political purposes, the trial He endured was not legally held according to Jewish law. He died for the potential benefit of every human being who has ever lived or ever will live. To enjoy the salvation and eternal life offered by God through Christ, a person must be a true Christian. Be prepared to spend time with any students who may feel the need to talk about these matters.

SESSION PLAN

BEFORE CLASS BEGINS: Photocopy the Compass worksheet and the Fun Page. Cut apart the "Witness Cards" on the Teaching Resource pages. It is not necessary to photocopy them. See the ATTENTION GRABBER for suggested materials.

Attention Grabber

ATTENTION GRABBER (3-5 minutes)

Materials required: Today's session is a mock jury trial. You, the leader, will be the "judge." If you wish, wear a robe (a choir robe would do nicely) and use a gavel or hammer. You will also need a cross to show your students. A sketch of a cross on butcher paper will suffice, but we suggest you bring a cross for students to handle, or even make a large one from scrap lumber. Finally, you need an "expert witness;" an older student or adult sponsor who can act as an expert on crucifixion (see the EXPLORATION).

When students are seated, show them the cross and say, **What is this?** When students respond, say, **What is its purpose?** Point out to your learners that indeed, the cross is a device used to kill. It is an instrument of death.

Explain, **Jesus died on a cross similar to this one. He didn't receive a fair trial, yet He allowed His own crucifixion. Today we are going to have our own trial. We are going to question some witnesses who saw Jesus die, and some who may have been responsible for His death. We will attempt to discover who the guilty person or persons really are. I will be the judge, and you will be the jury. Some of you will be the witnesses.**

Bible Exploration

EXPLORATION (30-35 minutes)

Distribute the Compass worksheet. Tell students, **I am handing out a "Trial Notes" worksheet. During this trial, you are all to write down what each witness says so that at the end of our trial you will be able to decide who is guilty. I'm also handing out "Witness Cards" to some of you. When I call for a certain witness to testify, whoever has that card will come up to the witness stand and tell what the card says.**

Step 1 (20-25 minutes): Hand out the "Witness Cards." Say, **This court is now in session. I call the first witness to the stand.** As the witness comes forward, explain, **There is no body to prove that someone died. But many witnesses claim to have seen Jesus crucified. We will now hear the testimony of some of those witnesses.**

The first witness is a representative of the chief priests and others who are mentioned in Mark 15:1. Instruct the witness to read the verse aloud (as it says to do on the "Witness Card"). Then, for a bit of "trial drama," ask a few questions such as, **So are you telling this court that you were there on the morning of the Crucifixion?** and **Tell us again, in your own words, who was with you and who you handed Jesus over to.**

The next witness is Pilate. Again allow the witness to follow the instructions on the "Witness Card" and again ask a couple of probing questions to make sure all students have the facts straight and have enough time to fill out the "Trial Notes" chart. Repeat this procedure until you have finished with the first eight witnesses (the chief priests, Pilate, the soldiers, Simon, the man with the sponge, the centurion, Mary Magdalene and Joseph).

Say, **We have now shown, beyond a reasonable doubt, that a death did occur.**

Jesus was crucified until dead, and His body placed in a tomb. I would now like to call an expert witness, Dr. Smith, who will describe in detail the nature of crucifixion.

When the witness is seated, ask the following questions, allowing the witness to respond from the "Witness Card."

1. **As you know, Doctor, it was the Roman government who executed people by hanging them on crosses. Was this execution reserved for the worst criminals?**
2. **How long did it usually take a person to die?**
3. **What was the actual cause of death for most crucified individuals?**
4. **Could you describe a typical crucifixion?**
5. **Why were people's legs broken?**

Say, **We have established that Jesus was crucified, and we have seen the horrible nature of such a death. It is now time to hear the testimonies of several witnesses who may be able to help us establish who is responsible for Christ's death.** Call witness number ten to the stand.

Allow witnesses number 10 through number 14 to testify, asking probing questions as you go along. When through, tell students that the court is taking a five-minute recess to evaluate the testimony.

Step 2 (3-5 minutes): Lead a quick discussion centered on the testimony of all 14 witnesses. Ask students their opinions on which people were actually involved in the Crucifixion.

Step 3 (3-5 minutes): Call the court back into order, and ask the fifteenth and final witness (Paul) to come forward. Introduce the witness and say, **Thank you for coming. You have written a**

large part of the New Testament, including portions that speak of the death of Christ. Would you tell us, in your own words, why Jesus died? Please read 1 Corinthians 15:3 and Romans 5:8 to us.

After the student reads both verses, say, **So what you are telling us is that Jesus died for sinners. In other words, it was the sinners** who created the need for Christ to sacrifice Himself? But Paul, just who are these sinners? Please read Romans 3:23 to this court. When the student finishes, say something like, **All have sinned! That means we are all guilty of the death of Jesus Christ. He died to save us from our sins. We are the guilty ones!** Dismiss the witness.

Conclusion and Decision

CONCLUSION (3-5 minutes)

Tell students to individually read 1 Peter 2:24 in their own Bibles. Students are then to fill in the "Verdict" section of the Compass worksheet.

Close in prayer, thanking God for Jesus' death that we might live. Tell students that next time you will all be taking a look at Christ's return to life, the reason there was no "dead body." Distribute the Fun Page take-home paper.

Your students may wish to see this solution to the Fun Page jigsaw puzzle. If you like, cut apart the puzzle on the Fun Page and glue the correctly arranged pieces to a piece of cardboard. Display it in your classroom.

Note: The next session, session 11, requires scissors, envelopes, construction paper and colored pens. See the ATTENTION GRABBER, EXPLORATION, and CONCLUSION for details.

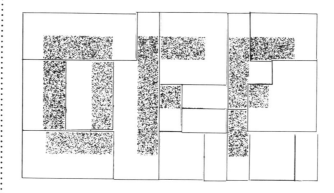

Trial Notes

Mark 15: The Death of Jesus Christ. Use this chart to record the testimony of all the witnesses in the trial.

Witness	Scripture	Testimony
#1 The chief priests	Mark 15:1	
#2 Pilate	Mark 15:2-15	
#3 The soldiers	Mark 15:16-20	
#4 Simon	Mark 15:21-32	
#5 The man with the sponge	Mark 15:33-37	
#6 The centurion	Mark 15:38,39	
#7 Mary Magdalene	Mark 15:40,41	
#8 Joseph	Mark 15:42-47	

#9 Expert witness' testimony about crucifixion:

#10 Man with shriveled hand	Mark 3:1-6	
#11 The chief priests	Mark 11:15-18	
#12 The Jewish leaders	John 5:8,9 and 16-18	
#13 Caiaphas	John 11:49-53	
#14 Teachers of the law	Mark 14:1,2	
#15 Paul	1 Corinthians 15:3, Romans 3:23 and Romans 5:8	

Verdict

Who is guilty of Christ's death?
Have you personally received the benefit of Christ's death?

☐ Yes   ☐ No   ☐ Not sure

☐ I want to. (If you check this, be sure to talk to your teacher after class!)

Teaching Resource

Witness Cards

Cut out these cards for use during the EXPLORATION. The cards will tell your students what they are to do when they are on the "witness stand." There are 15 cards, one of which is for an "expert witness" who should be an adult or at least a high school student. If your class has less than 14 students, you can give each student more than one card. Only one witness is a woman (Mary Magdalene) so some of the girls in your class will have to speak in deep voices!

WITNESS #1

The Chief Priests
You are a representative of the chief priests and others mentioned in Mark 15:1. Read that verse aloud when the "judge" tells you to.

WITNESS #2

Pilate
Read Mark 15:2-15 aloud when the "judge" tells you to.

WITNESS #3

The Soldiers
Read Mark 15:16-20 aloud when the "judge" tells you to.

WITNESS #4

Simon
Read Mark 15:21-32 aloud when the "judge" tells you to.

WITNESS #5

The Man with the Sponge
Read Mark 15:33-37 aloud when the "judge" tells you to.

WITNESS #6

The Centurion
Read Mark 15:38,39 aloud when the "judge" tells you to.

WITNESS #7

Mary Magdalene
Read Mark 15:40,41 aloud when the "judge" tells you to.

WITNESS #8

Joseph
Read Mark 15:42-47 aloud when the "judge" tells you to.

WITNESS #10

Man with Shriveled Hand
Read Mark 3:1-6 aloud when the "judge" tells you to.

WITNESS #11

The Chief Priests
Read Mark 11:15-18 aloud when the "judge" tells you to.

WITNESS #12

The Jewish Leaders
Read John 5:8,9 and 16-18 aloud when the "judge" tells you to.

WITNESS #13

Caiaphas
Read John 11:49-53 aloud when the "judge" tells you to.

WITNESS #9

The Expert Witness

The "judge" will ask you to respond to five questions about crucifixion. The answers are below.

1. The Romans could crucify anyone they wanted to, except Roman citizens. However, it was considered a form of execution fit only for the lowest form of "scum" and the most disreputable of criminals. During some civil uprisings just after the time of Christ, so many Jews were crucified in Jerusalem that there was a shortage of wood and space for the crosses! In Rome, the emperor Nero crucified hundreds of Christians, lighting them on fire.

2. Death rarely came before 36 hours, and sometimes a person could last as long as nine days.

3. The actual cause of death was usually suffocation. The position of the body on the cross put such pressure on the body that as the person weakened, the muscles necessary for breathing were unable to do their work. Also, fever caused by infection from the nails claimed many lives. Starvation was another cause of death.

4. The crucified person was stripped naked and secured to the cross by ropes or by a nail between the wrist and palms. The rope made death slower, because the person would not bleed and there was no risk of hitting a vein and causing a quick death. However, friends of the crucified person could come and cut him down during the night. Nails made it harder to remove the person alive. Incidentally, the threat of rescue is the reason why a centurion guarded Jesus. A nail was also usually driven through the feet. The position of the body put great pressure on the heart and arteries, causing the victim to experience the blinding pain of a headache within a few minutes of crucifixion.

5. People's legs were broken as a humanitarian act. Strange as this may seem, it is true. Breaking a person's legs allowed him to die more quickly, because he couldn't push up with his legs to relieve the pressure on his chest. To insure the person was really dead, they were then stabbed.

WITNESS #14

Teachers of the Law

Read Mark 14:1,2 aloud when the "judge" tells you to.

WITNESS #15

Paul

When the "judge" tells you to, read these two passages:

"Christ died for our sins according to the Scriptures."

1 Corinthians 15:3

"God demonstrates his own love for us in this: While we were still sinners, Christ died for us."

Romans 5:8

Then, again when the "judge" says to, read:

"For all have sinned and fall short of the glory of God."

Romans 3:23

FUN Pages!

Session 10

TURN SIN OFF!

Why did Jesus die? To take care of a major problem: SIN. Jesus turned off the problem of sin by His death on the cross. You also can turn sin off by working this jigsaw puzzle. Cut or very carefully tear the pieces apart and rearrange them to change the word "SIN" to the word "OFF." Hint: The puzzle is the same size and shape when it is correctly reassembled. If you're stumped, the person who gave you this game has the solution.

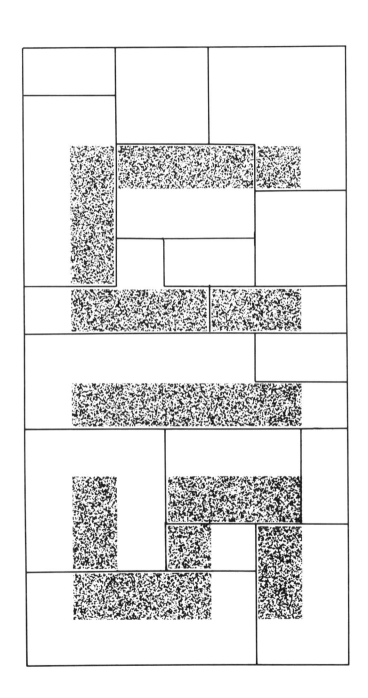

DAILY NUGGETS Wisdom from God's Word for you to read each day.

Day 1 Read Mark 12:41-44. How much money did the rich people give, and how much did the poor widow give? Who gave more?

Day 2 Mark 13:31. Heaven (atmosphere and space), may pass away, but what can we rely on because it lasts forever?

Day 3 Mark 13:32-37. What are some ways you can be prepared for Jesus' return?

Day 4 Mark 14:3-9. Why did the woman pour perfume on Jesus head? What did Jesus say about this?

Day 5 Mark 14:10,11. Who betrayed Jesus?

Day 6 Mark 14:12-26. What did Jesus do with the bread and the cup?

"He himself bore our sins in his body on the tree, so that we might die to sins and live for righteousness; by his wounds you have been healed."

1 Peter 2:24

THE COMPLETE JUNIOR HIGH BIBLE STUDY RESOURCE BOOK #2
© 1987 GL/LIGHT FORCE, VENTURA, CA 93006

THEME: The bronze snake on the pole reflects Christ on the cross.

Session 10

BIBLE STUDY OUTLINE

Read Numbers 21:4-9 to your audience. Make these remarks as time permits:

- Verses 4,5: This is an incident which occurred after the Israelites escaped with Moses from Egypt. They were running from centuries of slavery to the Promised Land—the country which God had promised to give them. But the people grew impatient with the way Moses and God were leading them. In fact, it was just a few days' walk from Egypt to the Promised Land—but it took them forty years because of their rebellious nature! Today, even Christians are sometimes impatient with God. By nature, we don't want to wait for Him, we want things to go the way we want them to go. The best lesson you can learn is that God does things the way He wants to do them. If you want to play on His team, you must play by His rules. Notice that the Israelites started questioning God's wisdom ("Why have you brought us up?"). "Why?" is usually the first thing a person says when he or she is spiritually "bombing out." We shake our bony little fists at God and ask, "Why?" But by faith we know that God works for the good of those who love Him (read Romans 8:28).
- Verse 6: So God pulled a fast one on the people who had apparently lost their love for Him; He sent poisonous snakes to bite them! A strange thing to do, but as we shall see, a thing that points us to Jesus Christ and His death on the cross.
- Verse 7: The people repented and asked Moses to pray that God would save them from the snakes. The word "repent" has two basic meanings: It means to "turn back," as in turning away from sin and returning to God; and it means "to change one's mind," as in deciding that a certain act or attitude is wrong and to stop doing it.
- Verses 8,9: Instead of removing the snakes, God gave Moses these unusual instructions. If a person was bitten, he or she could come to the bronze snake on the pole and be healed. Does this sound familiar? It should. In the very same way, we are saved from our sins—from spiritual death—by the death that Jesus died while hanging on a cross. If we come to Him, He saves us. If we don't

come to Him, we are as good as dead. Jesus referred to this bronze snake incident when He predicted His death (read John 3:14-16). Jesus promises eternal life to those who believe in Him.

OBJECT LESSON: SNAKE

As you speak, show your students a real or a toy snake.

DISCUSSION QUESTIONS

1. **Why do people sometimes grow impatient with God? What can we do when we feel impatient or upset with our Lord?**
2. **We have said that if we want to play on God's team, we must play by His rules. What would happen if you played on a professional football team, but went out on the field wearing what *you* wanted to wear—a tennis outfit? What happens when we break God's rules? Why does God establish rules for us to follow?**
3. **Why didn't God just kill the snakes instead of making Moses hang up a bronze one? Why doesn't God just make us perfect and sinless instead of requiring Jesus to die? Will we ever be perfect and sinless?**

A couple of games to help break the ice.

TELEPHONE EXCHANGE

Players form pairs. Each pair receives a copy of the telephone push button illustration below, upon which they write their first names and phone numbers. Players use their two telephone numbers to form as many words as possible. (Each digit translates into three letters, as shown on the dial. The digits "1" and "0" do not count.) Words formed must be at least three letters long. Remember, couples may **combine** their numbers to form words. Couple with the most words wins.

1	**2** ABC	**3** DEF
4 GHI	**5** JKL	**6** MNO
7 PRS	**8** TUV	**9** WXY
	0	

Player #1: Name _____ Number _____

Player #2: Name _____ Number _____

WHAT'S MY NAME?

Tape an index card to each player's back. Letter each card with a different Bible character. Each player is to determine what name is on his or her own back by asking questions of the other players, who are free to look at the cards. Questions can only be answered "Yes" or "No."

The first three players to correctly identify their names are the winners. Instead of Bible characters, you could do famous people, animals, or any other category you like.

His Resurrection SESSION 11

WHAT THE SESSION IS ABOUT
The Resurrection is the central event of Christianity.

SCRIPTURE STUDIED
Mark 15; 16, 1 Corinthians 15:12-20.

KEY PASSAGE
" 'Don't be alarmed,' he said. 'You are looking for Jesus the Nazarene, who was crucified. He has risen! He is not here. See the place where they laid him.' " Mark 16:6

AIMS OF THE SESSION
During the session your learners will:
1. Study the chronological order of the events surrounding the Crucifixion and Resurrection.
2. Understand the importance of the Resurrection to the faith of Christians today.
3. Thank God for the Resurrection.

INSIGHTS FOR THE LEADER

Today's session focuses on that joyful event, the resurrection of Jesus Christ. This is the event that sets the Christian faith apart from man-made religions. No other religion claims that God actually became a man, died, and then came back to life. The empty tomb of Christ is in sharp contrast to the smoldering remains of the founders of religions.

During the class time, your students will play a game which will help them understand the events surrounding the Resurrection, as described in the last chapter of Mark. The game—called "Resurrection Hunt"—will also review the Crucifixion, which was studied in the last session.

The Significance
After the game, you and your students will discuss 1 Corinthians 15:12-20. Paul speaks of the importance of the Resurrection, in response to some believers in Corinth who did not accept the doctrine of the physical resurrection of the dead. He wrote to show them that the resurrection of the believers is tied inseparably to the resurrection of Christ. If there is no resurrection for believers, there is no resurrection of Christ. And without Christ's resurrection, the Christian faith is futile, preaching is useless, and Christian believers are deluded and miserable. Happily, this is not the case, for Jesus *did* rise from the dead, and

His resurrection is the demonstration that we, too, shall rise.

After the Resurrection
Your students will discuss the significance of the events recorded in Mark 16 regarding the appearances of Christ after the tomb was found to be empty.

Jesus first appeared to Mary Magdalene, who went and told the mourning and weeping disciples (see vv. 9-11). They did not believe that Jesus had come to life. Neither did they believe the two disciples who saw Jesus while walking in the country (vv. 12,13).

Finally, Jesus appeared to the Eleven (Judas was gone, of course), and rebuked them for their lack of faith. From our modern perspective, it seems strange that these people could have seen the miracles Jesus performed—including raising the dead—and heard His repeated predictions of His own resurrection and yet still have had no faith. But then, we are used to hearing about the Resurrection; it is the central part of our faith. The disciples were caught by surprise.

Remember, too, that many people had witnessed the horrible death Jesus suffered. It was a violent end and would have made the death seem all the more irrevocable.

Lack of faith is still a major problem today. Young Christians such as your students are in

the process of learning what they believe. During your discussion time you may wish to stress the fact that the same power of God which raised Christ can work in any Christian's life on a daily basis, allowing that Christian to be an effective witness, efficient prayer warrior, and unwavering disciple. In the moments following the Crucifixion, the disciples had neither faith nor power—but because of Christ's resurrection, we are privileged to have both.

The Good News

When Jesus spoke to the disciples, He said, "Go into all the world and preach the good news to all creation" (v. 15). Because the disciples were obedient, and because all generations since then have obeyed, we today are saved Christians. Your students are included in Christ's command: they are to spread the gospel. Young people may not feel great confidence in their ability to spread the good news. Impress upon them that God doesn't expect them to save millions by this time tomorrow. Instead, tell your students that they can do simple things to spread the good news, such as inviting a friend to the next fun event at church or helping a friend to understand that God is not a cosmic killjoy who wants to slap harsh rules on everyone (something that many young people strongly believe). These simple things can be the first link in a chain that eventually leads to salvation for that friend.

Accompanying Signs

Your students will be interested in what Jesus had to say concerning miraculous signs accompanying believers: casting out demons, speaking in tongues, picking up snakes, drinking poison and healing people (see vv. 17,18). This subject is complex, as witnessed by the wide difference of opinions among modern believers. You may wish to do some research and put together a separate Bible study on the subject. For now, point out to students that these particular words of Christ were referring to signs that would prove the reality of God as the disciples spread the good news. The final verse of Mark, verse 20, makes it clear that these signs did occur as the disciples obeyed Christ. Today, as students learn to fully obey Christ, they will see God working in their lives—confirming to them the reality of God.

Power and Authority

Finally, Christ was taken up into heaven and sat at the right hand of God—the place of greatest authority, with the highest power in the universe. That power and authority belong to any person who belongs to Christ. That power and authority apply to our lives at this moment—and carry beyond into eternity. Because of the resurrection of Christ, we have confidence that we, too, will be raised from the dead and live forever with the Lord. We will enjoy a perfect existence without the pains or troubles of life on earth. The poor will have everything they need; the handicapped will be made perfect; the troubled will know peace and joy. Knowing what lies in our future can help us to live with hope and perseverance.

SESSION PLAN

BEFORE CLASS BEGINS: This session requires several envelopes and some photocopying and cutting of the three Teaching Resource pages. There is no Compass student worksheet this time. At the CONCLUSION, students will need construction paper and colored pens to make greeting cards. You may wish to supply candy bars or other rewards for those who finish the games first.

Attention Grabber

ATTENTION GRABBER (3-5 minutes)

Materials needed: The "Word Scramble" Teaching Resource page, prepared as described on the first page. Enough envelopes for every two or three students to have one.

When class begins, move students into groups of two or three. Give each group one of the sealed envelopes you have prepared and say, **Open your envelopes and solve the word scramble to discover the most important event in the history of mankind.** If you wish, tell students that the first group to finish will receive a reward.

If after two minutes no one gets the answer, give them the solution and make a transition to the next

part of the session by asking, **Why do you think some people would say that the Resurrection is the most important event in history?** After several have responded, say, **The Scriptures make it clear that the Resurrection is the focal point of Christ's ministry. If He had not been raised from the dead He would have been only a good teacher, or a fanatic. Just someone who lived and died a long time ago. But He was resurrected and lives today. Let's look at what else the Bible has to say about the Resurrection.**

Bible Exploration

EXPLORATION (25-35 minutes)

Materials needed: Copies of the "Resurrection Hunt" Teaching Resource pages, prepared as described on the page. Enough envelopes for each group of three or four students to have one.

Step 1 (15-20 minutes): Distribute the "Resurrection Hunt" envelopes that you have prepared, one to each group of three or four students (you may wish to combine groups that

NOTES

were formed for the ATTENTION GRABBER).

Explain, **Open your envelopes and pour out the contents. You will find 32 cards, each one representing an event which occurred during the crucifixion and resurrection of our Lord. The object of this game is to put the cards in the correct order in which those events occurred. You are not allowed to use your Bibles for this game! Later, we will open our Bibles and see the proper order of the events. This is a tough game; it will teach us as much about what we *don't* know about Christ's final days as what we do know. The cards are numbered, but they will not be in numerical order when the game is correctly solved. Work together in your group to come to a majority agreement regarding the placement of each card. The winning group is the one that comes closest to the correct order of events.** You may wish to offer a reward to the winning team.

Make sure everyone understands the rules, then allow groups about 15 minutes to play. When time is up, go over Mark 15 and 16 to find the proper order of events. Write the numbers of the cards on the chalkboard for all to see. The proper order is 9, 24, 3, 19, 29, 11, 1, 16, 23, 4, 32, 27, 21, 17, 6, 15, 20, 2, 8, 14, 22, 28, 18, 25, 5, 26, 30, 10, 7, 31, 13, 12.

Step 2 (10-15 minutes): Spend some time discussing the significance of some of the events surrounding the Resurrection, using the following suggestions:

1. The disbelief of the disciples (16:9-14). It's possible to spend a lot of time with the Lord yet not come to a point of complete trust and understanding. Christians must commit themselves to trusting God, a trust that will grow and mature over the years.

2. Christ's instructions to go and preach (v. 15). We owe our salvation to the disciples' obedience to this command. We also need to carry on the message, even if all we know how to do is invite a friend to the youth group meetings.

3. The signs accompanying the believers (vv. 17,18). Discuss with your students the nature and purpose of these signs.

4. The right hand of God (v. 19). This position indicates one of authority, the right-hand seat next to human kings is always reserved for the second in command, the "right-hand man." Jesus has all the power and authority of God, and that is why Christianity is the way and the truth.

Instruct students to turn in their Bibles to 1 Corinthians 15:12-20. Read the passage aloud, pointing out that Paul wrote this passage in response to some believers who did not accept the doctrine of physical resurrection from the dead. Explain to your learners that Paul is saying that without the Resurrection, Christianity is a complete waste of time. Everything depends on the fact that Christ was raised.

You may wish to point out that Christ's resurrection is the main thing that sets Christianity apart from man-made religions. No other religion claims that God became a man, died, and then came back to life. Mohammed, Buddha, and the rest are all in their tombs—Christ's is empty. (If a student asks about others who were brought back to life—as some Hindus claim, for example—tell the class that anyone brought back to life eventually dies again. Only Jesus never died again.)

Conclusion and Decision

CONCLUSION (5-7 minutes)

Materials needed: Construction paper and colored pens for each student.

Explain to students, **You are to create a greeting card telling why you are glad that Jesus Christ rose from the dead. Write this card as if you were sending it to God.**

When students are finished, tell them to keep the cards in their Bibles for a few days as a reminder of today's lesson. Close in prayer and distribute the Fun Page.

CREATIVE ALTERNATIVE (5-7 minutes)

Have students work individually to compose a song expressing their thanks or praise for the fact that Jesus was raised from the dead. Tell students to think of a popular song to which they can write their new lyrics. Instruct learners to keep their songs in their Bibles for a few days to remind them of today's lesson.

Close in prayer and distribute the Fun Page.

Word Scramble

Prepare a "word scramble" envelope for every two or three students in your class: Cut apart the letters of each "RESURRECTION" below and mix them up in an envelope (one set per envelope). Seal the envelopes. If you have a very large class, you may need to make extra copies of this page.

RESURRECTION **RESURRECTION**

RESURRECTION **RESURRECTION**

RESURRECTION **RESURRECTION**

RESURRECTION **RESURRECTION**

RESURRECTION

RESURRECTION

Resurrection Hunt

Photocopy these two pages, making enough copies for every three or four students to have one set. Cut out all the cards and place each set in an envelope.

As you can see, the cards are numbered. The numbers will help you reveal the proper order of the cards to your learners (the order is given in the EXPLORATION). Of course, the numbers are not in chronological order.

9. The Sanhedrin hands Jesus over to Pilate.	19. "Crucify Him!"	1. Jesus brought to the Place of the Skull.	4. "King of the Jews" posted over His head.	21. "He saved others, but He can't save Himself."
24. "Are you the king of the Jews?"	29. Crown of thorns.	16. Jesus crucified.	32. Two robbers crucified.	17. Darkness came at noon.
3. "Which shall I release— Barabbas or Jesus?"	11. Simon was forced to carry the cross.	23. Soldiers cast lots for His clothes.	27. "Come down from the cross."	6. "My God, My God, why have You forsaken Me?"

15. Sponge with vinegar.	14. Joseph buries Jesus.	25. Jesus appears to Mary Magdalene.	10. "Go into all the world and preach the good news."	12. The Lord works with the disciples, with signs and miracles.
20. Jesus breathes His last.	22. Three women bring spices.	5. Jesus appears to two disciples.	7. Jesus taken up into heaven.	
2. Temple curtain torn in two.	28. They saw the stone rolled away.	26. Jesus appears to the eleven disciples.	31. Jesus sits at the right hand of God.	
8. "Surely this was the Son of God!"	18. A man in white says, "Do not be alarmed."	30. Jesus rebukes the disciples for their lack of faith.	13. The disciples preach.	

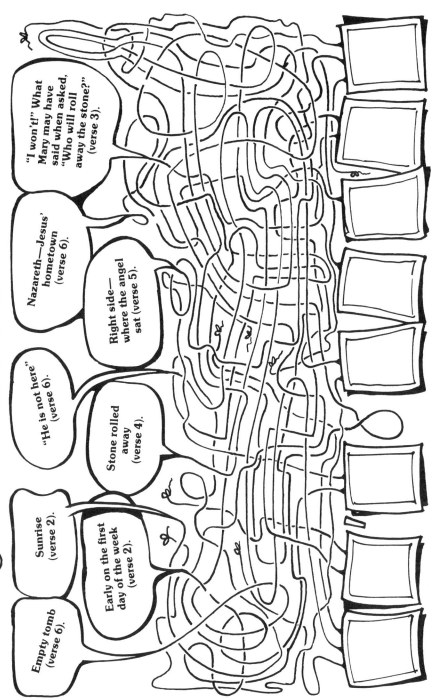

THE EMPTY TOMB

Session 11

Here's a game that will help drive home the fact that Jesus is alive— raised from the grave by the power of God. The cartoon balloons are connected to the squares by strings. Follow the strings to see which balloons attach to which squares. Then, take the first letter in each balloon and write it in the attached square. When you have finished, the squares will spell a simple but very important message. This game is based on Mark 16:1-7.

"I won't!" What Mary may have said when asked, "Who will roll away the stone?" (verse 3).

Nazareth—Jesus' hometown (verse 6).

Right side— where the angel sat (verse 5).

"He is not here" (verse 6).

Stone rolled away (verse 4).

Sunrise (verse 2).

Early on the first day of the week (verse 2).

Empty tomb (verse 6).

© 1987 GL/LIGHT FORCE, VENTURA, CA 93006

DAILY NUGGETS Wisdom from God's Word for you to read each day.

Day 1 Read Mark 14:32-36. How was Jesus feeling? What did He pray?

Day 2 Mark 14:37-41. What did Jesus ask His disciples to do? What did they do?

Day 3 Mark 14:42-50. Based on verse 49, why do you think Jesus allowed Himself to be arrested, instead of fighting back?

Day 4 Mark 14:55-65. What statement of Jesus did the high priest consider to be blasphemy?

Day 5 Mark 14:66-72. What did Peter do when the rooster crowed the second time?

Day 6 Mark 15:1-15. Pilate asked Jesus two questions. What were they and how did Jesus answer?

"'Don't be alarmed,' he said. 'You are looking for Jesus the Nazarene, He is not here. See the place where they laid him.'"

Mark 16:6

THE COMPLETE JUNIOR HIGH BIBLE STUDY RESOURCE BOOK #2
© 1987 GL/LIGHT FORCE, VENTURA, CA 93006

THEME: Jesus appeared to two disciples on the road to Emmaus—and He can appear to us today.

Session 11

BIBLE STUDY OUTLINE

Read Luke 24:13-35 to your listeners. As time allows, stress these points:

- Verse 13: Two disciples were walking away from the scene of Christ's crucifixion. They were downcast and dejected because the hopes they had placed in Jesus had been destroyed by His terrible death.
- Verses 14-16: Somehow, they did not recognize the Lord. Have you ever been depressed? Maybe you know how hard it can be to "recognize" Jesus when you're down and out. But that's the time we need Him most! [Do the OBJECT LESSON.]
- Verses 17-24: Jesus prompted them to talk to Him. They spilled the whole story, ending in a note of confusion about the lost body and the vision of angels.
- Verses 25-27: Jesus explains to them that the Old Testament had predicted many things concerning the Messiah—the one sent from God to save the people. Even with this explanation, the two still did not recognize Him. Today we see people who hear the words of this book, yet never recognize the life-changing truth it contains. Some of you at this Bible study may hear the truth now, yet leave without recognizing God. Don't be the one to make that mistake.
- Verses 28-30: We learn a very important lesson from Christ's behavior at the table. He was an invited guest, but notice that He did not act like a guest. He served the bread, which was the **host's** job in those days. It would be as if you invited a friend to a picnic but he brought the food, told you where to sit, what games to play and when to leave. In short, Jesus took over. And that is exactly what He expects to do in your life. You may think you're inviting Him into your heart as a guest—but He is no guest. He is God and He expects you to obey and honor Him as Lord and God.
- Verses 31-35: The two disciples couldn't fail to notice the similarities between Christ breaking the bread and what they had heard about the Last Supper (assuming neither was there). They hurried back to Jerusalem and told what they saw. Notice their change in attitude.

Before, they were depressed and down. But after recognizing Jesus, they were happy and alive. They probably jumped back to Jerusalem in three leaps! This is the same reaction we tend to have when we see Jesus in our hearts. He makes us happy and alive.

OBJECT LESSON: THE VEIL

Explain to your students that sin (rebellion against God, failure to follow Him) tends to create a "fog" that blinds us and makes it hard to "recognize" God. That's why it is important that Christians try to live for Jesus always, instead of being satisfied to let a few sins slip through. Show your students a curtain, veil, or blindfold.

DISCUSSION QUESTIONS

1. **Why do people need to turn to Jesus when they are down or depressed? What can He do for them?**
2. **Why did the Messiah have to die? Why is it so wonderful that He came back to life?**
3. **What was the significance of Jesus' breaking the bread?**
4. **Why do you suppose the disciples' hearts "burned" within them?**

Some icebreakers.

HIDDEN NAMES

Make up index cards as follows: Label cards 1A, 1B, 2A, 2B, 3A, 3B and so on (one number/letter combination per card) until you have enough cards for each player to have one. Distribute the cards randomly. Make sure both *A* and *B* cards of each number are distributed—you must have an even number of players to do this. (If necessary, allow an adult sponsor to play to keep things even). Caution students to keep their numbers SECRET.

When all cards are distributed, tell all players with *A* cards to line up near one wall, while *B* card holders line up near the opposite wall.

To play the game, shout a random number, such as five. The two players holding the 5A and 5B cards immediately raise their hands so they may be identified. The first player to correctly give the first name of the other player wins. If one player does not know the other's name, introduce them. The player who wins the round scores a point for his or her team. If one player does not immediately raise his or her hand when called, subtract one point from that team. After all have played, the team with the most points wins. If you wish to play the game again, have players exchange their cards within their own teams.

GUESS TEST

Play these simple guessing games:

1. **Guess the number of beans in a jar.**
2. **Guess the weight of a volunteer. (Bring a bathroom scale.)**
3. **Tell the participants your middle initial (or that of someone else) and let them guess your middle name.**
4. **Let them guess your age, or that of another adult sponsor.**

Winners receive small prizes. (The first two guessing games are won by the person closest to the truth.) If you like, have players write down their answers on paper which you then collect and read. This will cause the game to fill more time.

Peter's Denial

WHAT THE SESSION IS ABOUT

When we fail, Christ restores us.

SCRIPTURE STUDIED

Mark 14:26-31,66-72; John 21:15-25.

KEY PASSAGE

"Again Jesus said, 'Simon son of John, do you truly love me?' He answered, 'Yes, Lord, you know that I love you.' " John 21:16

AIMS OF THE SESSION

During this session your learners will:

1. Discover that Peter's failure did not ruin his relationship with Jesus.
2. Acknowledge that Jesus loves Christians even though they may fail Him.
3. Express ways in which Jesus might deal with their personal failures.

INSIGHTS FOR THE LEADER

In this final session, your learners will examine the account of Peter's denial of Jesus, and Jesus' restoration of Peter. Peter's denial is recorded in Mark 14, while the restoration is in John 21.

Failure Predicted

Jesus predicted that His disciples would desert Him like sheep scattering when the shepherd is removed. Peter evidently thought that was a terrible idea, and claimed, "Even if all fall away, I will not" (Mark 14:29). Then Jesus responded, "Today—yes, tonight—before the rooster crows twice you yourself will disown me three times." Peter again protested, saying, "Even if I have to die with you, I will never disown you." The other disciples said the same thing.

But when Jesus was arrested, "everyone deserted him and fled" (v. 50), true to the prediction. However, Peter and John did muster enough courage to follow Him into the courtyard of the high priest while He was being tried.

The Failure

A servant girl came by and recognized Peter as a follower of Jesus. Fear evidently took over, and three times Peter denied knowing his Lord. When Peter heard the rooster crow, he remembered the Lord's prediction, and he broke down and wept. (See Mark 14:66-72.)

This was a serious failure on Peter's part. He had been overly confident in his own abilities and his own courage. But his courage had failed him and he denied the Master who had captured his heart and his loyalty. His weeping demonstrates his sorrow and remorse at his own failure.

With many leaders, that failure would have ended the relationship. There would be no opportunity for Peter to be restored to fellowship and to a share of the work. But Jesus is not that kind of leader. With Him, failure is not the end of the story.

The Restoration

John tells of the restoration of Peter. (See John 21:15-25.) Many Bible students have felt that Jesus' threefold repetition of the question, "Do you love me?" gave Peter the opportunity to set aside his three denials of his Lord. Certainly the conversation gave him the occasion to show that he had learned something about himself and that he was a humbler man than the one who had boasted that he would never deny Jesus.

Jesus gave Peter a job to do: feed His sheep. In giving Peter this important assignment, Jesus indicated that Peter still had *value*. His failure had not made him a total loss as a

human being or as a servant of the Lord. It had hurt him and his Master, but it did not destroy his entire life or their relationship. He was to learn from it and go on from there, still in fellowship with Jesus and obedient to the task that had been given him.

The Message

This is an important message for your junior high students to learn. As they grow from childhood to adulthood, they will make mistakes and they will have failures. Fallen human beings, even those who are born again and enjoying fellowship with God, can't expect perfection from themselves. It is important to acknowledge mistakes and failures and sins, to confess them, to receive the cleansing and forgiveness that our Lord offers, and then to go on with life. It is not part of God's plan for young people to get so bogged down in their own failures that they can't do anything useful with their lives.

In some cases certain consequences of failure will remain. Sometimes these things will simply be a bad memory; sometimes it may be more serious, such as a physical injury or a friend whose feelings are hurt. God doesn't always immediately wipe out the natural consequences of failure. But He is always ready to receive and to forgive the person who failed, to restore that person to a productive relationship with Himself.

SESSION PLAN

BEFORE CLASS BEGINS: You will need a table lamp for the object lesson in the EXPLORATION. Photocopy enough Compass worksheets for each student to have one.

Attention Grabber

ATTENTION GRABBER (3-5 minutes)

When class begins, say, **I want you to think about a time when you really blew it—some failure, stupid mistake or idiotic thing you said or did. Draw a simple picture of what you did. Then answer these questions: How did people treat you? How did you feel about the way they treated you? Be prepared to share your picture and your answer if you are willing.**

As students work, tell them about a failure of your own. Ask for volunteers to share their pictures and answers.

Say, **Thank you for sharing about your failures. That's not always easy to do. Today we are going to find out about a time when Peter, one of the Lord's closest friends, failed Him in a pretty spectacular way. And we are going to see what happened to Peter after that.**

Bible Exploration

EXPLORATION (20-25 minutes)

Step 1 (3-5 minutes): Write the following headings on your chalkboard or overhead projector.

Mark 14:26-31

Jesus said:	*Peter said:*
Verse 27:	Verse 29:
Verse 30:	Verse 31:

Read Mark 14:26-31 aloud (or have a volunteer read). Then work together with your students to write down in the appropriate column what Jesus said and what Peter said.

Step 2 (15-20 minutes): Assemble students into groups of four or five. Distribute the Compass worksheet and tell students to work together to complete the assignment. Move from group to group as they work, offering suggestions and encouragement. Tell students that each should fill out his or her own worksheet with the part that he or she will read during the "newscast."

When students have completed assignments, have groups present their "newscasts." (Do as many groups as time will allow.)

CREATIVE SUGGESTION

If you have access to a video camera and recorder, tape the newscasts and allow students to view them during a tongue-in-cheek movie party. Make silly awards for several categories such as "Whitest TV Smile," or "Most Difficult to Understand," or "Biggest Giggler." Afterwards, show a good movie that your students can enjoy and discuss.

Step 3 (3-5 minutes): To help students understand why it is important to be restored following a sin or failure, perform this simple object lesson:

Plug a table lamp into a wall socket and turn the lamp on. As you speak about failure, walk away from the wall until the cord is pulled from the socket. Plug the cord back in so the light goes on again. Do this one or two more times. (Be sure to walk straight away from the wall so there is little strain on the cord.) Explain, **In order to function properly, the lamp must be attached to the socket. The power flows only when the lamp is attached to the socket. In the same way, a Christian who becomes separated from God by sin, or who blows it like Peter did, needs to be restored so that the power can flow. Without God's power in our lives, we cease to function properly.**

NOTES

Conclusion and Decision

CONCLUSION (3-5 minutes)

Write the word "fail" in the center of the chalkboard, like this:

F
A
I
L

Tell students, **Use the letters in the word "fail" to form new words telling what Jesus can do with your failures. Write words or phrases or whole sentences that begin with the letters *F, A, I,* and *L*. Be prepared to explain what you mean by the words you select.**

Let students work for a couple of minutes. Then ask for several to volunteer to explain their acrostics.

Summarize what students have said about Jesus' response to their failures. Close in prayer and hand out the Fun Page.

Note: Session 13 requires special materials. See page 173 for details.

Network News

Work together in your group to write a TV news report based on Peter's failure (Mark 14:66-72) and his restoration by Christ (John 21:15-25).

Use the headings below as a guide for your report. If you have time, complete the "Failures Anonymous Commercial" at the bottom of the page. Be prepared to share your "newscast" with the class by electing people to serve as the news reporter and the people who are interviewed.

Network News Introduction: "Good evening. This is the Network News brought to you by the kids at _____. In the news today . . ." [Write a lead-in to your report]

"Live" Interviews (based on Mark 14:66-72):

The servant girl:

Others standing near:

Peter:

The rooster:

Now your news reporter should introduce the events of John 21:15-25 by saying something like, "Yes, Peter failed. But late today, a shocking new development has changed everything. Jesus Himself appeared and spoke to Peter . . ."

Interviewer's questions (based on John 21:15-25):

Reporter: Jesus, could you tell us in your own words what you said to Peter and what he said to You?

Jesus: [see verses 15-19]

Reporter: What do you mean by "Feed My sheep?"

   What do you mean by "Follow Me?"

Conclude your newscast by explaining the significance of Jesus' telling Peter to work for Him and follow Him (indicating that Peter was restored to a place of good standing).

Failures Anonymous Commercial

Write a short commercial designed to appeal to Christians who have made mistakes, failed, or sinned. Your commercial should offer the solution, for example, the fact that God forgives sin and restores the sinner just as Jesus restored Peter.

Session 12

GULP!

As you know, Jesus can cure any disease. Well, here's a disease that you may be suffering from right now! It's very common—perhaps more common than the common common cold. Uh, you know what we mean, anyway. To find out what the disease is, use your pen or pencil to connect the dots. (Yes, we know dot-to-dot games are usually for little kids. But, after all, this one does have big numbers!)

Now that you've found the disease: This disease strikes when we say or do something foolish—which is a pretty common event. Happily, Jesus can restore us by His love and power. When we blow it, He is willing to stand us up on our own two feet—even if He has to remove them from our mouth first!

© 1987 GL/LIGHT FORCE, VENTURA, CA 93006

DAILY NUGGETS Wisdom from God's Word for you to read each day.

Day 1 Read Mark 15:22-26. Where was Jesus crucified? What did the notice say?

Day 2 Mark 15:29-32. Jesus refused to save Himself so He could save others. Have you received the salvation He offers?

Day 3 Mark 15:33,34. What did Jesus cry out? Compare Psalm 22:1,2.

Day 4 Mark 16:1-5. What did the women see when they came to the tomb?

Day 5 Mark 16:6,7. What did the young man tell them?

Day 6 Mark 16:9-20. What did it take for Jesus' disciples to believe He had risen?

HOT THOT

"Again Jesus said, 'Simon son of John, do you truly love me?' He answered, 'Yes, Lord, you know that I love you.'"

John 21:16

THE COMPLETE JUNIOR HIGH BIBLE STUDY RESOURCE BOOK #2
© 1987 GL/LIGHT FORCE, VENTURA, CA 93006

THEME: Failure and restoration.

Session 12

BIBLE STUDY OUTLINE

Read John 8:2-11 to your students. As time permits, make the following points:

- Verse 2: As was His custom, Jesus taught the people. He was a wonderful teacher, using object lessons from life to help the people see the truth about God. He also performed miracles to verify the truth of His words.
- Verses 3-6: Some of the religious leaders tried to trap Jesus with a tough situation. They brought the woman caught in adultery, but notice they did not bring the man. This was almost certainly a setup; they had probably used a man to trap the weak woman, and had allowed him to escape—all so they could trick Jesus into making a statement that would contradict the Old Testament law. Why? Maybe they were jealous of Jesus' powerful teaching and His popularity. Maybe they truly thought He was a dangerous heretic. Whatever the case, they did not trust God to deal with the situation. They decided to take matters into their own hands, and they did not care at all about the ethics of their action. Incidentally, they misconstrued Moses' law. Both the woman and the **man** were to be stoned, and only if some other special circumstances were involved. Verse 6: What did Jesus write on the ground? No one knows. Some say He may have been writing the sins of the people accusing the woman. We don't know.
- Verse 7: The people persisted, so He responded to them. His statement really took the wind out of their sails. They had all sinned. And because He had confirmed Moses' law by offering them the chance to throw a stone, they had no basis for accusing Him. Never try to win a battle with Jesus!
- Verse 9: They left, the old ones first (probably because they were wise enough to recognize their sins, and because they had the most sins!).
- Verses 10,11: Jesus did not condemn her. He did not throw a stone. Instead, He let her off the hook. But He told her to leave her life of

sin; in other words, to stop committing adultery. This is the same situation you and I face when we come to God today. Although we are guilty of sin, He forgives us and lets us off the hook. We fail, and He restores us. But notice that He requires that we stop living a life of sin. If you expect to be a Christian without making any changes in your behavior, you're going to find yourself in a jam. God expects a change.

OBJECT LESSON: THE BLANK TAPE

Show a cassette tape to your students as you talk about forgiveness and restoration. Tell students that our lives record our bad actions just as a cassette records sounds. But no matter how full our life becomes with sin, God can cancel out those sins and restore us—just as a tape can be erased and reused. (If you like, demonstrate with a portable cassette recorder.)

DISCUSSION QUESTIONS

1. **What sort of changes must a young person make when he or she becomes a Christian?**
2. **Is it possible to be a Christian if you are unwilling to make changes? Is it possible to be an effective Christian?**
3. **What do non-Christian friends think about you if they see you doing things that are wrong? What do they think about God?**
4. **Have you ever doubted whether God really loves you and wants to forgive you? If so, how does the story of the woman caught in adultery make you feel?**

THE COMPLETE JUNIOR HIGH
BIBLE STUDY RESOURCE
BOOK #2

Mud sports.

TUG-O-MUD

This, of course, is the original mud sport. Dig a ditch, fill it with water, mix it up real well to form lots of mud. Players then play a standard game of tug-of-war across the mud.

HERE'S MUD UP YOUR NOSE

Place a balance beam securely, as illustrated. Participants play "Robin Hood and Little John" on the beam, using foam-covered sticks or rolled newspapers.

A TRIP TO THE HAIRDRESSER

When everybody is good and muddy, let players style each other's hair with mud. Take lots of photos and make a poster for your youth room.

APPLE MUD PIES

Sit everyone around the mud and let them bob for apples with their feet (if the mud is thick, the apples will stay on the bottom). Player with the most apples wins.

His Birth

WHAT THE SESSION IS ABOUT

The birth of Christ

SCRIPTURE STUDIED

Matthew 2:1-18; Luke 1:26-45; 2:8-20,25-35; John 1:1-14.

KEY PASSAGE

"Today in the town of David a Savior has been born to you; he is Christ the Lord." Luke 2:11

AIMS OF THE SESSION

During this session your learners will:

1. Examine the announcements of Christ's birth given to selected individuals.
2. List specific responses to the announcements.
3. Indicate a personal response to God's gift of Christ.

INSIGHTS FOR THE LEADER

We call this a "Special Session" rather than Session 1 because we hope to encourage you to use this session during Christmas week, if Christmas is not too far away. If you do wish to save this session until then, begin this course with Session 1, which begins on page 00.

This course is a study of the life of Christ, taken primarily from the book of Mark. It makes sense to study His birth, but the event is not recorded in Mark! Therefore, this session relies on other Gospels.

His Identity

Your students will first examine John 1:1-14 in order to review the identity of this baby whose birth is so significant. (Session 1 goes into much more detail on Christ's identity.)

John 1:1-14 speaks of the Word who "was with God and . . . was God" (see v. 1). He is the Creator, the One who made all things. He became flesh and lived among us. He is the one and only Son, "who came from the Father, full of grace and truth" (v. 14). Thus, in a few short verses, the Son of God is identified in His deity and in His humanity. It is He, the Creator of the universe, who entered this world as a human baby in order to make a way for sinful human beings to be forgiven and to become children of the Father.

After this brief review of His identity, students will examine the accounts of His birth, focusing on the various people mentioned in the scriptural narratives and their responses to Him.

Mary, His Mother

Mary was in Nazareth when the angel Gabriel made his announcement to her: "Do not be afraid, Mary, you have found favor with God. You will be with child and give birth to a son, and you are to give him the name Jesus. He will be great and will be called the Son of the Most High" (Luke 1:30-32). Although Mary didn't quite see how she could have a child since she was a virgin, she readily submitted to God's will in the matter. This is an indication of the character qualities that were seen by God and that caused Him to select her for her important role in the birth of His Son.

Elizabeth

Mary's relative, Elizabeth, was an older woman who had never had a child. However, some six months before Gabriel's visit to Mary, the angel had visited Elizabeth's husband, Zechariah, and informed him that he and Elizabeth would have a child.

Mary went to visit Elizabeth, who lived in the hill country of Judah. As soon as Elizabeth heard Mary's greeting, she was filled with the Holy Spirit. She exclaimed, "Blessed are you among women, and blessed is the child you will bear! . . . As soon as the sound of your greeting reached my ears, the baby in my

NOTES

womb leaped for joy. Blessed is she who has believed that what the Lord has said to her will be accomplished!" (Luke 1:42-45).

The Holy Spirit had given Elizabeth special insight into the identity of Mary's baby, and so she worshiped and praised Him, at the same time blessing the woman selected to be His mother.

The Shepherds

The shepherds came into the picture after Jesus was born (see Luke 2:8-20). They were watching their flocks when an angel came to them and told them, "Do not be afraid. I bring you good news of great joy that will be for all the people. Today in the town of David a Savior has been born to you; he is Christ the Lord" (vv. 10,11). Then a large number of angels appeared, praising God.

After this startling experience, the shepherds decided to seek out the baby whose birth had been so amazingly announced. "When they had seen him, they spread the word concerning what had been told them about this child, and all who heard it were amazed at what the shepherds said to them (vv. 17,18). They also glorified and praised God for what they had heard and seen.

Simeon

When Jesus' parents took Him to the Temple when He was eight days old, a devout man named Simeon met the family. He took Jesus in his arms and praised God. He also prophesied about Jesus' future. God gave him insight to know that Jesus was the promised Saviour, and that His ministry would reveal the condition of people's hearts.

The Wise Men

Turning to Matthew 2:1-18, students will look at the wise men, who came from the East to find Jesus. They had a star that indicated to them that the king of the Jews had been born. They came to worship Him and to give Him valuable gifts.

Herod

Unfortunately, in the process of seeking out Jesus, the wise men did an unwise thing; they revealed to King Herod that an important personage had been born. Herod felt threatened. Instead of worshiping and loving Jesus, he wanted to get rid of Him, to kill Him. The wise men were warned by God in a dream not to go back to reveal Jesus' location to Herod. Enraged, Herod ordered the murder of all the infant boys in the Bethlehem area. Jesus' parents, also warned in a dream, fled to safety in Egypt. In the Scriptures for this session, students will see the responses of the various people to the birth of the Lord—submission, praise, worship, gift-giving, and, in the case of Herod, a desire to get rid of Him.

The point of the session is to encourage your students to determine their own responses to Jesus. They will have a chance to pick which Bible person studied best represents their own response to the living Son of God. And they will be given a moment to decide for themselves a practical way to express their response to God or others.

SESSION PLAN

BEFORE CLASS BEGINS: Students will be making Christmas decorations for your classroom (which you can store until the appropriate date, if necessary). The materials for the decorations are listed under the EXPLORATION heading. Make enough copies of the Compass student worksheet and the Fun Page for each student to have one, with extra copies for unexpected visitors.

Attention Grabber

ATTENTION GRABBER (5-6 minutes)

When students are seated, lead a brief discussion about when and where students were born. Ask them to relate the time of day, humorous circumstances, and so on. You might share one or two things about your own birth if needed to break the ice. (Be careful not to press any student to participate. Some may feel embarrassed about being adopted or born out of wedlock; others may not know details.)

Make a transition to the next part of the lesson by saying something like this: **We've been talking about the circumstances of our own births. Our Bible study today is going to enable us to explore the circumstances of the birth of Jesus Christ and how people responded to it.**

Bible Exploration

EXPLORATION (25-40 minutes)

Materials needed: You need construction paper, ribbons, glue, tape, glitter, marking pens, several scissors, and a few balloons.

Step 1 (4-5 minutes): Distribute the Compass worksheet, and copy the "Birth Announcements" chart onto your chalkboard or overhead projector. Say, **Take a look at the "Birth Announcements" chart on your Compass worksheet. As we read the Bible references on** the chart, **we will discover several people who had some amazing experiences when Christ was born. We are all going to work together to fill out this chart. I will write the answers on the chalkboard, and I want you all to write the answers on your copies of the Compass. Who will volunteer to read the first reference, Luke 1:26-38?** Work the entire chart, allowing different volunteers to read each Scripture portion.

173

NOTES

Note to *Step 4*: You can store inflated balloons in a freezer. Just kidding! Balloons will have to be redone for the Christmas party.

Your students may wish to see this solution to the Fun Page puzzle.

(If you like, write the solution on an extra copy of the Fun Page and pin it to your classroom bulletin board.)

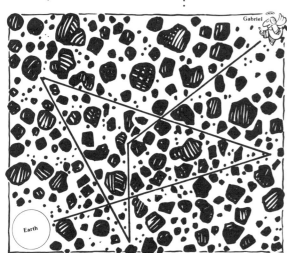

Suggested answers appear in this illustration:

Step 2 (3-5 minutes): Sum up the charts, and discuss the meanings and significance of the answers in the "Response?" column of the chart.

Step 3 (10-20 minutes): Provide the decoration materials to your students. Explain, **We are now going to decorate our room in celebration of the birth of Christ. Work in groups of three to five to create posters, banners, and anything else you can think of to liven up our room. Your decorations must be about something we learned just now from the Bible. Some of you might want to put one of the Bible verses we studied on a banner. Others can blow up the balloons and draw faces on them with the markers. King Herod would be a fun balloon face to make. Give him a paper crown and an ugly expression! Whatever you make, make it fancy and fun. Use the ribbons and glitter to make your projects as attractive as possible. All projects must reflect at least one important thing we've learned from the Bible today.**

Step 4 (5-10 minutes): When students have completed their assignments, have them post them around the room. Discuss the meaning and significance of each project. Congratulate students for their efforts. If Christmas is still some time away and you wish to reuse these decorations at that time as a reminder of today's lesson, tell students you will take down and store the decorations until then. Otherwise, allow students to remove decorations when class is through.

Conclusion and Decision

CONCLUSION (3-5 minutes)

Direct students to locate the "I Can Identify" section on the Compass. Tell them, **We have seen how various people responded to the birth of Christ. The wise men worshiped Him and brought gifts. The shepherds praised God and spread the word. Herod wanted to kill Him. On the Compass, circle the character that comes the closest to representing the way you feel about the birth of Christ. Then, in the space provided, tell something you could do to express this response in a practical way to God or others.** Students are to do this individually.

When your learners have finished, close in prayer and distribute the Fun Page. Ask a few volunteers to stay behind to help pick up any scrap materials.

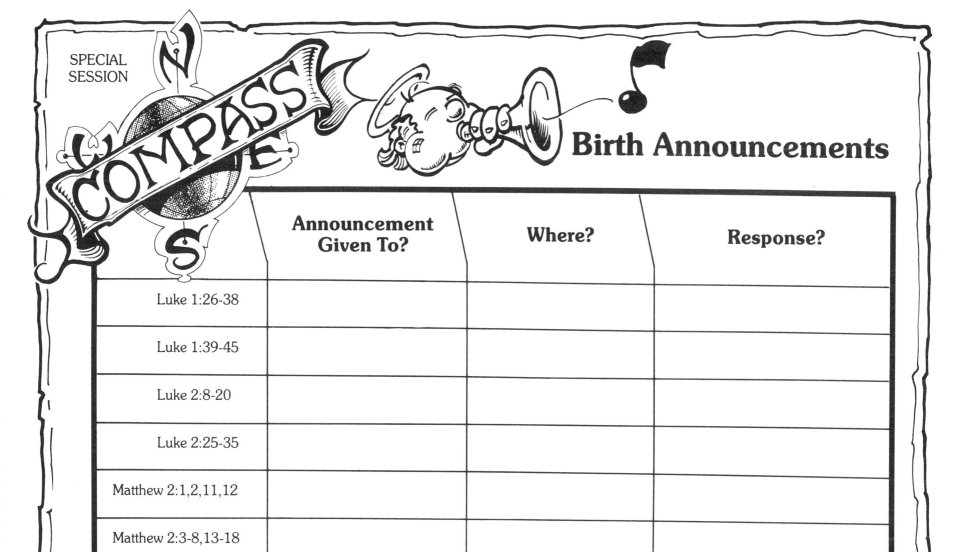

COMPASS

Birth Announcements

	Announcement Given To?	Where?	Response?
Luke 1:26-38			
Luke 1:39-45			
Luke 2:8-20			
Luke 2:25-35			
Matthew 2:1,2,11,12			
Matthew 2:3-8,13-18			

I Can Identify

Circle the character who best describes your response to the birth of Christ. Then tell what you could do to express this response in a practical way to God or others.

Mary

Elizabeth

Wise men

Shepherds

Simeon

Herod

BEELINE!

When Christ was born, the angel Gabriel announced His birth to several different people. Just for fun, you can help Gabriel fly a straight beeline with his message from heaven to earth. Here's how: Use a ruler or other straightedge to draw five connected **straight** lines from Gabriel to the Earth. An example of the idea is shown below. Your lines must be straight, they must be connected, and they must not touch any asteroids. Lines must be at least one inch long. Hint: Lines can cross.

Special Session

Example:

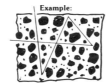

Gabriel

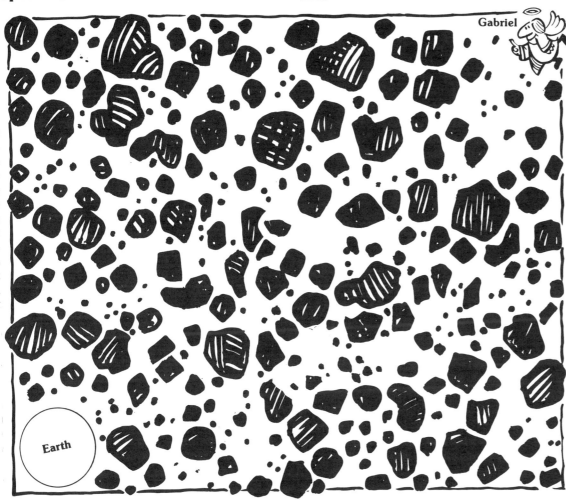

Earth

DAILY NUGGETS

Day 1 Matthew 2:1-13. What evil thing did Herod plot? Why do you suppose he did so?

Day 2 Matthew 2:13-23. This passage tells us that three predictions recorded in the Old Testament were fulfilled. What were the predictions? Why is it important that these predictions were fulfilled?

Day 3 Luke 1:26-33. Why was Mary afraid? What do you think you would do if an angel appeared to you?

Day 4 Luke 1:39-41. What do you think it means to be filled with the Holy Spirit?

Day 5 Luke 2:8-14. What does the word saviour mean to you?

Day 6 Luke 2:25-32. Simeon was called righteous and devout (in verse 25). What do those words mean?

"Today in the town of David a Savior has been born to you; he is Christ the Lord."

Luke 2:11

THE COMPLETE JUNIOR HIGH BIBLE STUDY RESOURCE BOOK #2
© 1987 GL/LIGHT FORCE, VENTURA, CA 93006

THEME: God can work through young people.

Session 13

BIBLE STUDY OUTLINE

Tell the story of young Jesus in the Temple, found in Luke 2:41-52. Make the following points as time allows:

- The Feast of the Passover (v. 41) celebrated that time in the Old Testament when God delivered Israel from the last plague in Egypt (the death of the firstborn) and their deliverance from bondage. The blood of lambs was involved in the original night of Passover, and Jesus would eventually shed His blood as the Lamb of God to save us all.

- His parents didn't miss Jesus at first (v. 43-45) because the caravan was large. Jesus was probably like any twelve year old— curious and no longer under constant parental supervision. Many teenagers insist on riding in the back seat of the car when Mom or Dad drives, even if there is room in the front. If cars were long enough, the kids would disappear into the distance!

- This twelve-year-old boy amazed the well-educated teachers (vv. 46,47). He understood things well beyond the grasp of most young people. (At this point, read Jeremiah 1:4-7, emphasizing the fact that God can use young people in mighty ways—if they are interested in serving God. Now go to the OBJECT LESSON.)

- His parents responded like most parents would (Luke 2:48)—except most parents would probably have beat Him and put Him on restriction!

  "I had to be in my Father's house" (v. 49). Jesus knew who His real Father was, and He was dedicated to obeying Him and doing His will.

  Then Jesus returned with His parents, was obedient to them (v. 51), and continued to grow mentally, physically, spiritually, and socially.

- Conclude by going over the DISCUSSION QUESTIONS and again making clear that God's power is available to those interested in serving God.

OBJECT LESSON:
POWER IN SMALL PACKAGES

Bring a portable circular saw to class. (Borrow it, if necessary.) Also bring some wood, such as a scrap of plywood. Tell students that this small tool has the amazing power to cut this wood in two in just seconds of time. Tell students you will now demonstrate this power. WITHOUT PLUGGING THE SAW IN, attempt to cut through the wood with a sawing motion. Of course, little will happen. Act confused. Students will point out that you need to plug it in, and you can make the point that a Christian needs to be plugged in to God to receive the sort of power young Jesus had and that Jeremiah referred to. IF YOU ARE EXPERIENCED at using the saw, plug it in and cut the wood (use eye protection); if you are not experienced, simply describe what would happen if the saw had electrical power.

Be sure to emphasize the need of power in a young Christian's life, then return to the final points of the BIBLE STUDY OUTLINE.

DISCUSSION QUESTIONS

1. **Why were the teachers amazed at Jesus? Where did His wisdom and understanding come from?**
2. **What is the source of wisdom and understanding for us today? [The Bible.]**
3. **Jesus wanted to spend His time at the Temple. How would your parents respond if you started spending a ton of time here at church?**
4. **Why do you suppose the Bible emphasizes that Jesus obeyed His earthly parents (v. 51)?**
5. **Why do we need God's power? What sort of things should we be doing with it? What could you do at school, for example?**

THE COMPLETE JUNIOR HIGH
BIBLE STUDY RESOURCE
BOOK #2

Games for Christmastime.

CHRISTMAS POINTERS

Give points to anyone who:

1. Wore red, green, or both.
2. Wore bells.
3. Has completed all his or her Christmas shopping.
4. Took someone to visit a store Santa.
5. Gave money to a Salvation Army (or similar) person.
6. Bought a card for a friend.

CHRISTMAS PINATA

Allow participants to make their own pinata for the upcoming Christmas party. Make papier mache with newspaper and paste made of flour and water. Use two bowls for forms, drying the paper in a low temperature oven. After filling the pinata with candy, tape the two paper halves together, forming a sphere. Decorate the sphere with colored paper, forming a face, body, or whatever the participants choose.

THE SLIME WHO STOLE CHRISTMAS

Participants are to bring wrapped presents to exchange. Gifts are to be inexpensive, and can be "joke" gifts. People choose the gifts randomly, not knowing what they are. After opening the presents, participants then sit in a circle. The person with the birthday closest to the date of the class meeting is the first to be the "slime." The "slime" has the opportunity to "steal" any other player's present; that is, he or she can demand any present from another player, in exchange for the present the "slime" is currently holding. The player on the "slime's" left now gets a chance to steal any present. Go around the room until all players have had a chance to steal gifts. Continue this until all players have had a chance to be the "slime." Game's over! Players keep the gifts they have.

Each participant then has the opportunity to "steal" any other player's present; that is, he or she can demand any present from another player. The "slime" gets to keep both presents—momentarily, at least. The next player now gets to steal any present. Go around the room until all players have had a chance to steal gifts. If anyone is left giftless, let him or her steal again. Continue this until all players have one gift—even if it's not the one desired!

CLIP ART AND OTHER GOODIES

The following pages contain all sorts of fun, high quality clip art. Put it to good use: brighten up your youth group's mail outs, bulletins, posters, and overhead transparencies. Cut 'em out, paste 'em up, run 'em off, and there you have it!

You'll be happy to know that the LIGHT FORCE publishes two great clip art books: the original YOUTH WORKER'S CLIP ART BOOK and the famous SON OF CLIP ART! Both books are available at your local Christian supply store, or write

THE LIGHT FORCE
P.O. BOX 6309
OXNARD, CA 93031

WANT TO PRODUCE GREAT PROMOTIONAL MATERIAL? TURN THE PAGE FOR EASY INSTRUCTIONS.

EASY INSTRUCTIONS

1. Get a sheet of clean white paper. This will become the master for your promotional piece.

2. Choose the art you want from this section. Cut it out and glue it to the master.

3. Add headlines with rub-on letters (available at any art store) or with a felt pen. Add body copy with a typewriter or by hand. (Type on a separate sheet and cut and paste.)

4. Run off as many copies as you need, hand them out or drop them in the mail. Presto!

TIPS:

Go heavy on the artwork, light on the copy. A piece with too many words goes unread.

Get in the habit of making a monthly calendar of events. It doesn't have to be an expensive masterpiece; just so it tells your group members what they can find at your church.

Print the calendar on the back of the **Fun Pages.** This will insure that those pages are saved and reread.

POOL PARTY

POOL PARTY

POOL PARTY

VALENTINE DAY

VALENTINE DAY

WAH!

ICE CREAM Social

WAH!

ICE CREAM Social

WAH!

ICE CREAM SOCIAL

185

Sign-Up Sheet
Please print your name, address, and phone.

NAME _____ PHONE _____

STREET _____

CITY _____ STATE/PROV. _____ ZIP _____

NAME _____ PHONE _____

STREET _____

CITY _____ STATE/PROV. _____ ZIP _____

NAME _____ PHONE _____

STREET _____

CITY _____ STATE/PROV. _____ ZIP _____

NAME _____ PHONE _____

STREET _____

CITY _____ STATE/PROV. _____ ZIP _____

NAME _____ PHONE _____

STREET _____

CITY _____ STATE/PROV. _____ ZIP _____

NAME _____ PHONE _____

STREET _____

CITY _____ STATE/PROV. _____ ZIP _____

NAME _____ PHONE _____

STREET _____

CITY _____ STATE/PROV. _____ ZIP _____

MORE GREAT THINGS FROM THE LIGHT FORCE!

OUTRAGEOUS OBJECT LESSONS

Your students' attention will be riveted on the truth of God's Word when you take advantage of these wonderful object lessons. Ranging from the very simple to the outrageous, from the classic to the unique, these lessons will greatly increase the retention time of your messages.

THE YOUTH WORKER'S BOOK OF CASE STUDIES

Over fifty true stories with discussion questions.

Nothing grabs a student's interest like a true story focused on the real problems and situations young people face today. Your Bible talks take on a new dimension of interest and impact when you spice them up with these terrific object lessons and true case studies.

Subjects range from abortion to gossip to self-image and beyond.

If you want over one hundred great ideas to liven up your own teaching times, you'll want OUTRAGEOUS OBJECT LESSONS and CASE STUDIES!

Order now from your local Christian supplier, or call us toll free.

800-235-3415 (Outside California)   **800-227-4025** (California only)

191